Best TEA SHOP WALKS *in* WORCESTERSHIRE

Irene Boston

Published by Sigma Leisure – an imprint of
Sigma Press, 1 South Oak Lane, Wilmslow, Cheshire SK9 6AR, England.

British Library Cataloguing in Publication Data
A CIP record for this book is available from the British Library.

ISBN: 1-85058-646-2

Typesetting and Design by: Sigma Press, Wilmslow, Cheshire.

Cover: The River Severn, Telford's Bridge, Bewdley

Maps and photographs: the author

Printed by: MFP Design and Print

Walks checked by: Mr R W Furlong

Disclaimer: the information in this book is given in good faith and is believed to be correct at the time of publication. No responsibility is accepted by either the author or publisher for errors or omissions, or for any loss or injury howsoever caused. Only you can judge your own fitness, competence and experience.

Contents

Walk 23. Waseley and Beacon Hill   105
Distance: 5 miles.

Walk 24. Worcester City   109
Distance: 4 miles.

Walk 25. Wyre Forest   114
Distance: 5 miles.

Locations of Walks

MAP SYMBOLS

९ ९ ९	Mixed woodland
⋔ ⋔ ⋔	Conifer woodland
G	Gate
S	Stile
CG	Cattle grid
FB	Footbridge
CP	Car park
✝	Church
PO	Post Office
PH	Pub
T	Toilets
═══	Road
⊬⊬⊬⊬⊬⊬⊬	Railway
BR	British Rail station
⌐	Hedge/field boundary
〰〰〰	River/stream
▦▬	Canal
⬭	Pond
	Fort/earthworks
Δ	Triangulation point

An Introduction to Worcestershire

If you stand on top of Worcestershire Beacon, the full spread of a county Sir Arthur Quiller-Couch called the "pastoral heart of England" is laid out before you. The view stretches as far as the Clent and Lickey hills, a welcome area of open country before the suburbs of Birmingham. Bredon Hill rises across the flat sweep of the Vale of Evesham and forms a solid rampart protecting the Cotswold escarpment. To the north-west, the distinctive outline of Abberley Hill can be seen above the lush beauty of the Teme valley. On clear days, the towers of Worcester Cathedral and the much smaller Pepperpot in Upton upon Severn glow in the sunshine.

Three major rivers wind their way through Worcestershire. The Severn effectively carves the county in two, while the Teme and Avon feed this mighty waterway on its journey to the sea. The Avon meanders around Evesham and Pershore in great loops as if it can't decide what to do, while the Teme flows gently through a wide valley to join the Severn at Worcester.

For such a relatively small county, there is a remarkable diversity of scenery which it no longer has to share with Herefordshire. Fortunately, the unhappy and ill-matched marriage between these two was finally granted a decree absolute on 1st April 1998. Some of Worcestershire's charms are obvious. Most people will include the Malverns, Severn Valley, City of Worcester, Wyre Forest and the Vale of Evesham in their itineraries. But a wealth of hidden corners is just waiting to be explored; lush woodland, meandering streams, undulating hills and picturesque villages.

Black and white half-timbered buildings typify the county but you are just as likely to come across Cotswold stone as elegant Georgian buildings. The Vale of Evesham and the Teme valley are renowned for their spring blossom nurtured by the fertile soil. The county's coat of arms contains a pear tree, an image which originally appeared on the banners of Worcestershire soldiers who fought at the Battle of Agincourt.

The Tea Shops

Who would dare disagree with Rudyard Kipling who once wrote "We haven't had tea for a week. The bottom is out of the Universe!" Drinking tea has long been one of our more enjoyable pastimes, almost a British institution. Originating in China, tea was not introduced to Europe until 1610 by the Dutch East India Company but is now grown in over 30 countries. Charles II became a devotee and was largely responsible for the popularity of tea drinking at court. However, the price of tea remained way beyond the purse of the average family, so smuggling and black market sales were common. Less scrupulous traders mixed the tea with all manner of unsavoury items, including clay, molasses and sheep dung, but this isn't something you'll find in any of the tea shops featured here!

The prospect of tea and a gooey cake is a wonderful temptation to look forward to at the end of a walk. It's been known to get my feet moving on more than one occasion, as my husband dangles the promise of a cream tea in front of me, like a donkey with a carrot. These days you are likely to find as much variation in the location and decor of a tea shop as you are in its menu. We visit tea rooms in craft centres, farm shops, gardens, a hillside well, Country Park and Forestry visitor centres, Cathedral cloisters, silk studios, a Victorian railway station and an old Merchant's House, as well as the more traditional venue, tucked away in a cosy cottage.

Tea shops are more commonly found in the popular villages or towns of any county, and you will find a similar concentration in Worcestershire's honeypots. All the tea shops in the book were written to, and later visited, by the author. Research can be hell sometimes! All extend a welcome to walkers, but please be considerate. Don't tramp muddy boots across their carpets, or knock crockery flying with a laden rucksack. Either wipe your boots, or better still, remove them.

Children are welcome but dogs won't, in the interests of hygiene, be admitted. In nearly all tea shops, there is some choice for vegetarians. Telephone numbers are provided so you can check opening hours. Even during the preparation of this book, opening dates changed and several tea shops closed altogether while new ones opened. Finally, these heartfelt sentiments from Sydney Smith say it all, "Thank God for tea! What would the world do without tea? How did it exist? I am glad that I was not born before tea".

The Walks

The walks, which range from 3 to 9 miles, offer a tremendous variety of scenery and walking conditions. Most of the routes are ideal for a half day stroll or a more leisurely day walk and meander through a gentle landscape of woodland, river valleys, villages and farmland. Several hill walks are included but the nature of the terrain means that these don't present the same challenge as peaks further north. None of the walks is too demanding even if you are not super fit and, where possible I've included a shorter option. Your only problem will be all the extra calories consumed in the tea shops! Remember, too, that many paths can become choked by summer growth which, on a hot day, can be tiring and mentally quite dispiriting.

There's no need to dress as if you're about to scale the Eiger but a few sensible precautions will ensure you enjoy the walk, rather than suffer through it. Good walking boots and waterproofs, along with a rucksack are essential. Obviously for walks 7 and 24 you can get by in shoes. A supply of liquid is vital, particularly on hot days, and a sun hat, insect repellent and sun cream will all add to your comfort. Extra layers of warm clothing are useful in the winter, particularly on the hills which can be much colder than the valleys. Gaiters are also useful in winter, if only to avoid my trick of finishing each walk with trousers plastered in mud from the knees downwards. A stick can be a great help in clearing nettles or fending off aggressive dogs.

Binoculars and pocket identification books of birds, trees and flowers, can greatly enhance your enjoyment of a walk. Glimpses of wildlife are a highlight of any walk and an ideal way of introducing children to the joys of nature. But the chances of close encounters with wildlife depend as much upon your own behaviour as on being in the right place at the right time. If you walk head down, chattering away, any wildlife will rapidly vanish. Even if you don't make a noise, most creatures have acute hearing and eyesight far superior to your own. Next time you're in woodland during spring, try this. Stand unobtrusively on a path, or better still by a tree. Keep quiet and watch intently for five minutes. Gradually, the birds will become accustomed to your presence and will go about their business as if you weren't there. If you must move, do it slowly. Sudden movement is as startling to wildlife as a loud noise. It can be helpful to have a rudimentary knowledge of bird song. Several tapes and CDs are available and remembering their calls is not as bewilderingly difficult as it first appears. Binoculars have other unexpected uses for walkers. They can help locate the position of a distant stile or waymark, or warn you if yonder herd of cattle contains a bull!

On the overall map you can see that the walks are in clusters. The locations of the walks depended on where the tea shops were, and some areas were bursting with eateries. But there are inevitably gaps where tea shops are thin on the ground and I haven't included every possible tea shop, particularly those in towns. Some tea shops are in areas where any attempt at a country walk would have degenerated into an obstacle course due to the state of the footpaths. One in particular is now surrounded by so much tarmac, you would need the speed of Linford Christie (with or without lunchbox!) to safely negotiate the new bypasses. And there was a surprising lack of response from some establishments. It seems that even in these tough commercial days, free publicity is not always welcome.

The directions were correct at the time of writing (1998) but the countryside changes all too frequently. Hedges are ripped out with depressing regularity, paths diverted and even complete bypasses built across footpaths. Stiles become gates and vice versa. Within a month of walking one route, all the stiles had been replaced by gates – a great improvement, but it made a nonsense of the original directions. It is vital to carry an OS map and both the Landranger and Pathfinder map numbers are given for each walk. Pathfinders are particularly useful as they show field boundaries – essential when you're not sure which side of a hedge to walk. But many Pathfinders have not been updated for years, and are now being replaced by the new Explorer series. So far, only one Explorer has been published which covers the Malverns and Bredon Hill.

Please note that where the directions read "head half right or half left" this assumes you are standing with your back against the gate or stile you have negotiated. Most of the footpath network in Worcestershire is in fairly good shape. In some popular areas, excellent route waymarking and regular use mean that the path is clear underfoot but there are still corners where poor waymarking has led to irregular use and, consequently, overgrown paths and rickety stiles. If I encountered any difficulties, these were reported. I hope that when you follow in my footsteps, any problems will have been ironed out. If you encounter any fresh difficulties, please write to the Rights of Way Officer, Dept. of Environmental Services, County Hall, Spetchley Road, Worcester, WR5 2NP.

As several of the walks use paths alongside the Severn or Avon, it should be borne in mind that these riverside tracks may flood in the winter or after heavy rain. At such times, roads in the area can also be affected, bringing chaos to traffic and local residents. During the devastating floods of Easter 1998, several tea shops and footpaths in this book would have been accessible only by canoe. Any flooding may affect walks 2, 3, 9, 20, 21, 22, and 24 alongside the Severn and walks 6 and 16 by the Avon.

The Wychavon Way

This medium-distance footpath runs for 42 miles from Holt Heath to Winchcombe in neighbouring Gloucestershire. You will see its distinctive "W" crown waymark as it crosses Bredon Hill on walk 1 and at its beginning on walk 9.

The Severn Way

When complete, this long distance path will follow the course of the Severn, Britain's longest river, from its infancy in the Welsh mountains to the Severn estuary. The boat most commonly used on the river was a flat-bottomed trow with square sails and the path waymarks depict this vessel.

We encounter several other medium-distance footpaths on our wanderings. The North Worcestershire Path, waymarked with a pine cone symbol, runs for 26 miles from Major's Green in the east to Kingsford Country Park in the west. We follow sections of it on walks 11 and 23. The Worcestershire Way, marked by a pear, stretches for 50 miles from Kingsford Country Park to Hollybush at the southern end of the Malverns. We meet it on walks 3, 13 and 20. We also use part of the Cotswold Way on walk 4 from Broadway.

Severn Valley Railway

Left to the tender mercies of Dr Beeching and without the dedication of a group of railway enthusiasts, the line between Kidderminster and Bridgnorth would have disappeared completely. Today, the Severn Valley Railway is one of Worcestershire's most popular tourist attractions. Volunteers operate the stations and act as guards on both diesel and steam services. As well as offering a marvellous day out, the railway provides a useful connection with the British Rail network at Kidderminster. The line also opens up the possibility of linear walks, taking the train to one station and walking back, or vice versa. Trains run every weekend throughout the year and on weekdays between May and October. A "Freedom of the Line" ticket, which allows you to get on and off at any station, is particularly good value. (Tel: 01299 403816 for information or 01299 401001 for 24 hour timetable).

Worcestershire Wildlife Trust

The Trust cares for nature reserves throughout Worcestershire and, largely through the efforts of its members and volunteers, aims to protect vulnerable areas from development. Details of membership from Lower Smite Farm, Smite Hill, Hindlip, Worcester, WR3 8SZ Tel: 01905 754919.

Public Transport

The car, and man's reliance upon it, is in danger of irrevocably damaging our countryside. Successive Governments have presided over the dismantling of our public transport system and people in many rural areas have little choice but to use their cars to make any journey. Public transport in Worcestershire is by no means excellent but it is improving all the time, and will continue to do so if we all play a part in increasing the demand for services.

Whilst I have provided car parking details for each walk, I would urge everyone to try out the bus and train services. All the walks are accessible by public transport. I have listed the main services but these change fairly frequently and it would be safer to check first. Bear in mind that services on Sundays and Bank Holidays are very limited and sometimes non-existent. Timetables can be obtained from the Council, Tourist Information Centres and libraries. The Great Britain Bus Timetable published by the Southern Vectis Bus Company, Newport, Isle of Wight is invaluable. The following numbers will help with specific enquiries: bus information 0345 125436, national rail enquiries 0345 484950, National Express 0990 808080.

Finally, I am grateful to the owners of all the featured tea shops who were extremely helpful and unfailingly enthusiastic. Thanks are also due to my husband, Rex, who accompanied me on every walk and to our friend, Rod, who can nettle bash with the best of them! I hope you enjoy the combination of good walking, delightful scenery and mouthwatering food. Meanwhile, having eaten far too many delicious cakes lately, I'm going on a diet!

Walk 1. Beckford and Bredon Hill

Start/parking: Beckford Silk Centre car park, grid reference 981 360. Please ask permission first and remember the Centre shuts at 5.30pm and is closed on Sundays and over Xmas. Alternative parking is possible in Beckford on the street near the church.

Distance: 6 or 9 miles.

Summary: An exhilarating walk to the top of Bredon Hill, where the longer option offers a full circuit of the upland plateau. Either route will reward you with marvellous views. Generally well waymarked with good paths and 9 stiles on short route and 11 on long.

Maps: Landranger 150, Explorer 14.

Public transport: Daily buses (except Sundays or bank holidays) from Tewkesbury, Cheltenham and Evesham (also the nearest railway station with buses stopping outside). Buses call at both Beckford and Ashton under Hill so you can join the walk at either point.

The Tea Shop

The Coffee Shop, Beckford Silk Centre, Beckford.

The Coffee Shop is inviting and airy with startling, colourful murals on the walls, which deceive the eye, making the room appear much larger than it really is. The simple menu offers delicious home-made soup, quiche and salads plus a mouth-watering selection of home baked cakes. The menu changes frequently with different specials on offer and wine and beer are available at lunchtimes. Access is via the shop and fascinating workshop area where you can watch the hand printing of textiles such as scarves and ties. Founded over 20 years ago, the centre produces a range of exquisite handprinted silk. Open Monday to Saturday 9.00am-5.30pm all year except Xmas and New Year. Tel: 01386 881507.

Parson's Folly, Bredon Hill

The Walk

From the Silk Centre, return to the road and turn left to Beckford village. At the T-junction, turn right to the church. Situated on the southern side of Bredon Hill, Beckford's architecture is reminiscent of the Cotswolds. Golden cottages are scattered along wide streets which boast a dazzling display of daffodils in spring. Join an alleyway at the rear of the churchyard to emerge onto a farm lane.

Turn right up the lane to houses where the lane bends left. At the end of the buildings, turn right through a double gate with a barn on the right. Follow this lane uphill, climbing gradually – the splendid views behind are ample excuse for a breather. Continue for a mile, over several path crossroads and through an avenue of trees. The lane eventually bends right, by a pheasant pen and leaves the trees to go through a gate. Turn left, by a blue arrow, and alongside the top edge of the pen. The path swings right to go through a gate.

Aim half right in the general direction of the mast at the top of the hill. The old fort lies to the left, its contours becoming clearer as you climb. Pass left of a copse of trees and head for the left corner of ruined barns. Go through the gate and keep ahead, with the wall on the

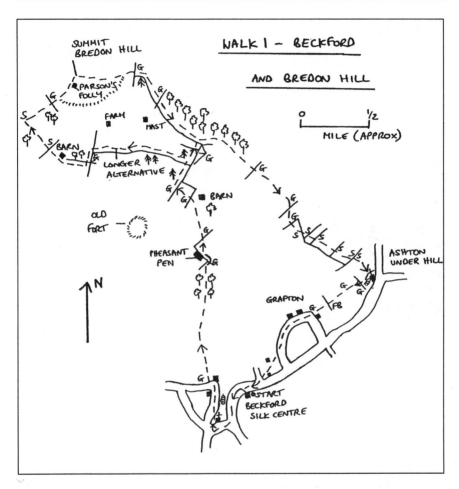

right. Go through the next gate and turn right alongside a wall by a belt of pine trees. Go through the next gate where you can choose either the long or short route. For the **shorter return**, continue ahead, trees on the left, to go through two gates in quick succession and turn right. This is where the longer route rejoins (**).

However, it would be a pity to miss the summit, so, for the **longer route**, turn left on a wide track past conifers. Ignore paths left and right and after passing farm buildings away to the right, go through a gateway to a T-junction of tracks. Turn left and after the next gate, turn right alongside a belt of trees. Walk past a barn and take a stile on the right into a field. These summit fields remain one of the few reliable places in Worcestershire to see hares. Rabbits are plentiful but these larger animals with black tipped ears and powerful hind legs are far more elusive.

Keep the wall on the left to the top corner. Cross the stile and turn right. Follow the fence through a stand of trees into a field, (the escarpment edge is on the left). Keep the wall on the left and go through a gate to the summit and the remains of a hill fort, which used the natural defensive contours of the escarpment. In the centre is the squat 18th century tower of Parson's Folly. Built by Mr Parsons of nearby Kemerton village it is now festooned with electrical gadgets. In the hollow by the tower, is the Banbury Stone, which resembles an elephant, depending on the angle you view it from. Legend has it that if the elephant hears the bells of Pershore Abbey, he will lumber down to the Avon for a drink!

The breathtaking view evokes Housman's description of "the coloured counties" – a patchwork which covers all of Worcestershire. To the west, the Malvern ridge beckons with the blue haze of the Welsh hills beyond. The eye sweeps round to the sparkle of the Severn estuary below the dark slopes of the Forest of Dean while the Cotswold escarpment occupies the entire southern horizon, punctuated by a prominent Broadway Tower. When you have drunk your fill, walk parallel with the wall on the left in a big right-hand curve to a gate by a stand of trees. Go through the gate, and follow first a wall, then a fence on the right to another gate.

Go straight through and walk between a belt of trees (left) and a fence (right). These stubble fields, particularly in winter, provide a marvellous habitat for mixed flocks of finches including yellowhammers, as well as the rarer brambling and corn bunting. Eventually this path meets the Wychavon Way, and our **shorter return (**)**. Ignore the Wychavon Way going left and keep ahead to the end of the trees, to go through another gate.

Follow the track ahead alongside the edge of the escarpment (wall on the left). Take the path as it curves right and go through a gate by a signpost. Follow the grassy track downhill through scrub to a yellow waymark. Cross the farm track to go through a metal gate with yellow arrows. Head half left, aiming for a stile halfway down the hedge. Cross the stile and head half right, still downhill to cross another stile.

Cross the narrow field to another stile ahead and go straight across a large field, passing right of a lone tree on the horizon. A marker post appears ahead but a stile in a dip has to be crossed first. Over the lip of the hill, Ashton under Hill church appears. Drop downhill, go straight over a sunken green path to a stile in the far fence. Cross the lane and go over two stiles into a field.

Head downhill to the church of St Barbara, the patron saint of gunners, blacksmiths and miners. Ashton under Hill is a charming blend of Cotswold stone and typical "magpie" timbered buildings. After your visit, return to the field behind the church and turn left alongside a pond. Go through a gateway and head half right to a gate just left of the houses ahead. Turn right along the lane. Within a few metres, where the lane curves right, go left on a rutted track across a field. Continue, with the hedge on the right, to cross a footbridge.

Head straight across the grass to a gate, just right of houses, and go straight ahead through Grafton. Follow the road as it bends left to reach a signpost into a field. This path is often unclear underfoot but aims left of the first house and right of the second. Then find the most convenient gap in the tree line beyond to reach the lane and turn right to the Silk Centre.

Walk 2. Bewdley and Dowles Brook

Start/parking: Plenty of car parking in Bewdley, usually ample space in
Gardner Meadows car park, off Severnside South. The walk
starts outside the Merchant's Tea Rooms by the bridge, grid
reference 787 755.

Distance: 5 miles.

Summary: A marvellous walk alongside the river Severn to the heart of
the Wyre Forest. Take your binoculars to see the wealth of
wildlife, particularly in spring when the woods around Dowles
Brook are alive with birds. Care needed with route-finding in
the woods; there is plenty of mud plus 4 stiles.

Maps: Landranger 138, Pathfinder 952.

Public transport: Regular buses from Bridgnorth, Kidderminster and Stourport
on Severn but no Sunday service. British Rail to Kidderminster
then catch the Severn Valley Railway to Bewdley – at
weekends and in the summer this is by far the best way to
arrive!

---

21 JAN 2000 – Excellent walk – must do again
Cold / sunny / 2hrs .   ## The Tea Shop

The Merchant's Tea Rooms, Severnside North, Bewdley.

Situated overlooking the bridge across the Severn, the tea room occupies the Merchant's House which was built out of profits from river trade. In the 19th century, it was the "King of Prussia" inn run by the Millward family, who were also coal dealers. You can no longer buy coal at the Merchant's House but a wide range of home-made food is available. The beamed ceiling, wooden tables and old prints decorating the walls offer a cool and welcoming haven on a hot day.

Jacket potatoes, toasted sandwiches and salads should satisfy the largest appetite. Other temptations include a Merchant's cream tea special when a sandwich and scones can be supplemented by teacakes, crumpets, and waffles with jam or maple syrup and ice cream. A delicious range of home-made cakes, including that wondrous invention, the non-fat chocolate cake, should fill any remaining corners. Open 10.00am-5.00pm in summer, closing at 4.00pm in

Merchant's House Tea Room

winter. They also give away a leaflet about places of interest in Load Street. Tel: 01299 402436.

The Walk

Bewdley's past history is inextricably linked with the River Severn. During Bewdley's days as an inland port, a lucrative trade developed transporting wool, coal and wood to Bristol. The arrival of the railway signalled the decline of Bewdley as a port but it was really the construction of the Staffordshire and Worcestershire canal that ended Bewdley's river trade. Ironically, Bewdley had refused to have anything to do with the "stinking ditch" so the canal was linked to the river a few crucial miles further south at Stourport.

The current bridge over the river, the fourth on the site, was built by Thomas Telford in 1798. Previous bridges have succumbed to the untamed power of the river. There are still relatively few roads across the fast flowing Severn, and during times of flood, it can bring the entire area to a standstill. Our winters are not as severe as they

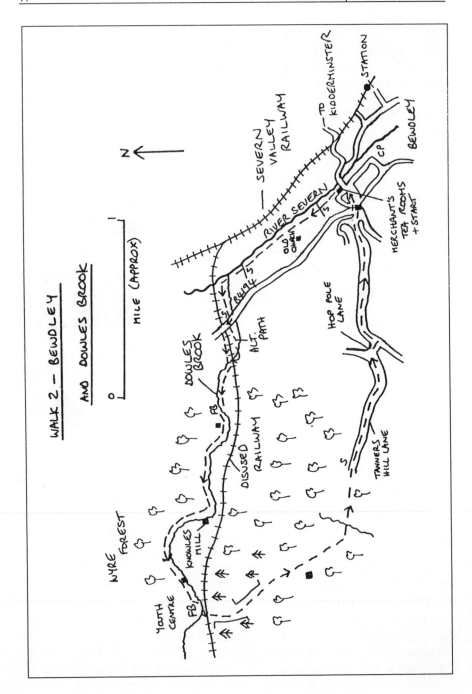

once were and the Severn no longer freezes. In the past, winter fairs were held on the ice.

Over the centuries Bewdley has been the centre for numerous traditional trades such as the making of ropes, baskets, besoms, coracles, wheels and clay pipes, to name but a few. Many of the street names hide fascinating stories. Dog Lane derives from Duck Lane because the town's ducking stool once stood at the end of it. Bark Lane would seem to indicate a connection with Dog Lane, but it's really so named because many tanners lived there.

Prime Minister Stanley Baldwin was born in 1867 at Lower Park House and became MP for Bewdley, succeeding his father. Tickenhill Manor was originally in the hands of the powerful Mortimer family whose later descendant, Edward IV, granted a charter to the town. In 1499, Prince Arthur married Catherine of Aragon by proxy at the Manor. Following Arthur's death, his funeral cortege rested at Bewdley en route to Worcester Cathedral while Catherine, in the manner of all politically expedient marriages, soon married his brother, Henry VIII.

From the Merchant's House, turn left along Severnside North, formerly called Coals Quay, where coal from Highley Pit further upstream was unloaded. Warehouses flanked the river and this quiet stretch would have been the scene of feverish activity as boats were being loaded. At the Mug House, men would negotiate and seal contracts with a mug of ale, which may explain the phrase "being taken for a mug". Follow the riverside path through gardens, and over a stile to walk alongside a fence. In the field on the left is the site of the old Dowles church, demolished in 1956.

Cross another stile by the piers of the old railway bridge. Turn left, alongside Dowles Brook to cross a stile onto the road. Turn right and, with extreme care, walk along the road for 100 metres. Cross and follow the bridleway ahead. (If this is too muddy, join the permissive path along the top of the railway embankment. This line, closed in 1964, once linked the Severn Valley line at Bewdley with the line at Ludlow. After a quarter of a mile, where a lane crosses the railway, go down steps and turn right down the lane to rejoin the bridleway).

Continue west on the bridleway, and where the lane forks, bear right and cross a bridge over Dowles Brook. This follows the county boundary with Shropshire but I won't tell anyone if you won't! This valley, with the water meandering through the Wyre Forest, is particularly rich in bird life. Heron, kingfisher, grey wagtail and dipper depend upon this fast flowing, unpolluted stream for food. Kingfishers nest in the high, sandy banks of the deeper reaches. Dippers, the only birds able to walk underwater, prefer the faster-flowing stretches and can frequently be seen hunting for insects. You can read more about the Wyre Forest and its wildlife in the last chapter.

Walk past a house and continue along the muddy lane, keeping Dowles Brook on the left. After a mile, pass Knowles Mill, presented to the National Trust in the 1930s. Continue past the next gate by an English Nature sign and then past Coopers Mill Youth Centre. At the next fork, by another sign, bear left and cross the footbridge. Turn right alongside Dowles Brook, now on the right, and after the path begins to climb, look for a yellow arrow on a tree. Follow the path left, climbing away from the brook to emerge on the old railway.

Cross over to join a footpath, past another sign. Ignore a path (left) and continue, with a fenced area first to the right, then on the left. Ignore the wide track branching right, and continue ahead. Where another waymarked path crosses yours, continue ahead past arrows on the trees until an open field and houses appear on the right. Pass left of these and at the end of the path, reach a rough lane.

Turn left over a stream. At the next corner, leave the lane and follow the path parallel to the lane. Cross a drive and follow another short section parallel to the lane, and over a stile at the end. Follow Tanners Hill Lane ahead, where delightful views extend across the valley. The lane drops downhill and then climbs to a T-junction. Turn right along Hop Pole Lane, and at T-junction turn left downhill into Bewdley.

Walk 3. Bewdley and Ribbesford Woods

Start/parking: Plenty of car parking in Bewdley and usually plenty of spaces in Gardners Meadows Car Park on Severnside South, grid reference 788 753, where the walk starts. Alternative parking at Blackstone Meadows Country Park car parks on both sides of Severn, see map.

Distance: 4 or 7 miles

Summary: A marvellously varied circuit, following the Worcestershire Way south from Bewdley to Ribbesford church before climbing into Ribbesford Woods. Return alongside the River Severn where the path can be a battle against summer growth. There is a short stretch of road and you'll cross 14 stiles on this well waymarked route. The shorter route avoids most of the riverside jungle and has 3 stiles.

Maps: Landranger 138, Pathfinder 952.

Public transport: Same as for Walk 2.

The Tea Shop

Beaulieus, Severnside South, Bewdley.

A mere scone's throw from the river Severn, Beaulieus occupies an elegant building and the tastefully decorated interior is very welcoming. The tables occupy two levels and you can sit overlooking the river but, fortunately, Beaulieus is high enough to escape the floods. Beverley and Christine Groves took over the tea room in November 1997 and it has been completely redecorated. The service is prompt and cheerful, and the prices are reasonable.

All the usual favourites are offered including home-made soup, cream teas, jacket potatoes and omelettes. An interesting choice of specials changes daily and a good range of sandwich fillings will appeal to children. Breakfast is served on weekend mornings and Sunday lunch has proved extremely popular. An impressive choice of delicious home-made cakes, including coffee and walnut, apple and sultana, is always available as well as muffins, crumpets and toasted tea cakes. Various ice-cream sundaes would tempt even the most dedicated dieter. Opening times vary; currently from 9.00am-5.00pm every day in summer and 10.00am-3.00pm on weekdays, and till 5.00pm at weekends in winter. Tel: 01299 402205.

Riverside gardens and Telford's bridge

The Walk

Return to the car park entrance and turn left down Lax Lane. At the T-junction, turn right and in 50 metres, turn left down an alleyway to join part of a Worcestershire Way circular walk. Ignore the first right, and at a T-junction, turn left past a pond and through a gate to follow the path on the right by the fence. On reaching a lane by a cattle grid, ignore the two paths to the right and continue ahead up the lane.

At the end, cross the road and continue down the bridleway to go under the bypass to Ribbesford. Home Farm and the onion-topped Ribbesford House have been converted into apartments. Go through the churchyard, climbing the steps at the rear. In summer, look for spotted flycatchers which nest in the surrounding trees and use the gravestones as launching posts to catch insects for their youngsters. St Leonard's with its half-timbered tower is well worth a visit.

Pause a moment at the top of the steps to appreciate the church's delightful setting in this wooded valley and to get your breath back! Cross the stile and puff your way to the top of the field and a strategically placed seat. Looking back, a glorious view unfolds to the distant Clent hills and Blackstone Rock, which we shall pass later. Continue into the wood and follow the clear path up the right edge of Ribbesford Woods. Owned by Forest Enterprise, the woods extend over the slopes of Stagborough Hill. The network of forest roads and footpaths wind through large areas of conifers and broad-leaved trees. The open rides allow flowers and butterflies to flourish and birdlife is abundant.

Cross a stile at the end of the wood, walk past the house and climb another stile. Go up the drive to a road. The tree stump is all that remains of The Gospel Oak, under whose branches John Wesley preached. This noble tree was felled in a storm in 1990. Turn left along the road for half a mile, (the Worcestershire Way goes off to the right). Gaps in the hedge allow views across to the tower blocks in Dudley. Where the road turns right by Glebe Cottage, go ahead past a barrier into Ribbesford Woods.

Continue on the forest road and after half a mile, there is an opportunity for a **shorter return**. At a footpath marker on the left, turn left off the forest road and follow the path downhill. Go straight over another forest road and continue downhill. On reaching another path, turn left, still downhill to a forest road, where you turn right. When the road starts to bend left, continue ahead on a narrow path which reaches the B4194 by the Woodman Inn, and turn left to meet the longer route at (**).

For the **longer route**, continue on the forest road for a mile amid the conifers, then through a cleared area with Stagborough Hill to the left. At a metal gate, bear right past a marker post and walk just inside the fence. After 50 metres, cross a stile on the left into a field and turn right. Go past a gate by yew trees and follow the hedge to climb a stile at the end of the field by a ruined cottage.

Continue with the hedge on the right over the next long field. In the distance, you can see four trees poking high above the rest in Shrawley Wood. These are the famous Wellingtonia trees and you can really only appreciate their height from a distance. When you're standing under them, you can't see the wood for the trees, so to speak! Climb a stile by a gate and continue down the track.

Go over a stile on the left and turn right along the hedge. Where the track bends right, walk ahead to enter the trees past a marker post. Walk downhill, and right of the hedge in front. Just before the corner, cross a stile on the left and turn right along the fence. Cross another stile and the B4194. Turn right and in 20 metres, turn left (not through the gate) along a permissive path through troublesome summer growth to the Severn.

Turn left and follow the riverside path which, although clearly defined, does become swamped with nettles and head high summer growth. At times, it can seem more like the banks of the Zambezi with Livingstone just round the next corner! Listen for the buzzing calls of sand martins which make their nest burrows in the sandy river banks (of the Severn that is, not the Zambezi), and can be seen hawking for insects over the water. Continue for over a mile to the playing fields of Bewdley Town Football Club and the road beyond, where the **shorter route** joins (**).

Walk along the road with extreme care for half a mile. At a left bend, turn right to rejoin, with some relief, the riverside path through Blackstone Meadows Country Park. The sandstone caves on the opposite bank at Blackstone Rock have been used variously as a hermitage and as shelter for travellers while they waited for the river to recede to allow them to ford it. Today, you are more likely to see climbers clinging like Spiderman to the sandstone rock. The path goes under the bypass bridge and in about a mile, passes the cricket pitch to reach the car park. Beaulieu's Tea Room is a little further along Severnside South.

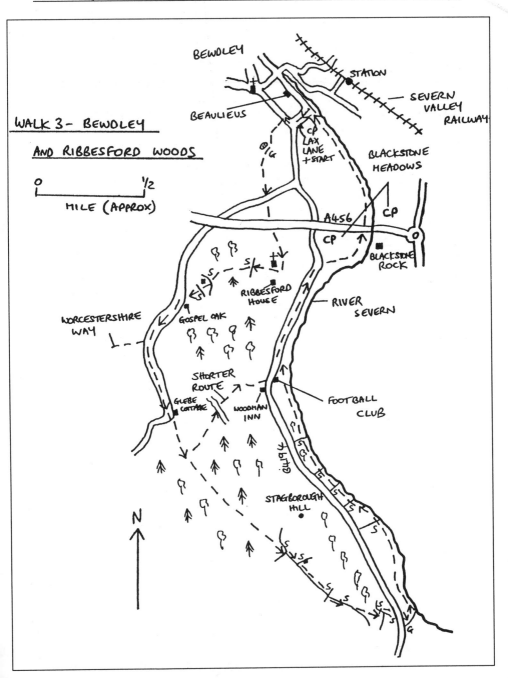

WALK 3 - BEWDLEY
AND RIBBESFORD WOODS

0 |—————————| 1/2
MILE (APPROX)

Walk 4. Broadway Tower

Start/parking: Several car parks in Broadway. Directions start from outside Tisanes, grid reference 095 375.

Distance: 4 miles.

Summary: A genuine taste of hill walking on excellent footpaths visiting Broadway's old church before climbing steadily to a superb viewpoint at Broadway Tower. Return along part of the Cotswold Way. As you would expect on the edge of the Cotswolds, this walk is well waymarked with 13 stiles.

Maps: Landranger 150, Outdoor Leisure Cotswolds Map 45, Pathfinder 1043.

Public transport: Regular buses from Stratford upon Avon, Bourton on the Water, Moreton in Marsh, Cheltenham and Evesham. No Sunday service. Nearest British Rail connections are at Moreton in Marsh and Evesham.

The Tea Shop

Tisanes, The Green, Broadway.

Tisanes, overlooking the village green, has been run for the past three years by Jill and Barrie Parmenter. The front half of the shop is Barrie's domain where he sells an amazing variety of loose teas and ground coffees, while glass cases display a remarkable collection of tea pots. The tea room, run by Jill, is at the rear and tables spill over into a sheltered garden, bright with flowers. What lifts this tea room out of the ordinary is the diverse menu, offering a variety of sandwiches with exotic fillings, including hot bacon, brie and avocado. A bewildering array of cakes such as carrot cake, apple janette and a wicked coffee and chocolate pyramid dessert are on offer. Speciality beverages include hot chocolate in various guises, with either a cream topping, brandy and a combination of coffee and hot chocolate, or you could try the spiced tea. More substantial fare of ploughman's, quiche and salad, together with soup in winter complete a tempting range.

Everything is obtained locally and freshly prepared. If you ever thought a tea cake was a small snack, try these – they're about the size of a small loaf! The atmosphere is cosy, everything is spotlessly clean, and the service is welcoming and attentive. For the sake of the carpet, please remove any muddy boots. You can always leave boots and rucksacks safely out of the way, just ask Jill. Open: 10.00am-5.00pm Monday to Saturday (closed Thursday) and 11.00am-5.00pm on Sundays from November to May. From June to October, 10.00am-5.30pm Monday and Saturday and 11.00am-5.30pm on Sunday. Tel: 01386 852112.

Cottages in Broadway

The Walk

To many visitors, Broadway is the epitome of the Cotswolds. However, it actually stands just inside the Worcestershire boundary, at the foot of the Fish Hill escarpment. The main street is indeed a "broad way", lined with golden cottages and wide pavements flanking a street which is sadly all too often choked with traffic. In a way, it's too popular for its own good. During summer weekends, Broadway positively buzzes with visitors so its considerable charms are best appreciated out of season.

Broadway is surrounded by marvellous walking country and many walks, both long and short, can be enjoyed. Broadway owes much of its early growth and prosperity to the coaching era in the early 1600s. It stood at a convenient point on the long journey from London to Worcester and in preparation for the steep haul up Fish Hill, the horses would be changed. This led to the establishment of various coaching inns. At one of them, the Lygon Arms, both Cromwell and Charles I stayed – although perhaps not at the same time, and certainly not at today's prices!

From outside Tisanes, turn right along the main street until you reach a signpost to the old church, opposite the Horse & Hound pub. Go down the alleyway, passing, as the sign says, "swings and things". Go through the gate into a field, head for and cross the footbridge ahead. Keep the fence on the right to go through another gate. In the next field, go through a gate, just right of a tall tree. The path is clearly defined as it passes right of the hedge ahead, then heads for the top right corner of the field to a lane. Turn left to the old church of St Eadburgha. The steps are a mounting block for horse riders.

Join a muddy bridleway opposite the church, signed Broadway Tower, which climbs through trees. Ignore gates to either side and at a T-junction, turn right over a stile by a gate. The path bears left uphill across grassland, passing right of a bungalow. Cross a stile and at the next junction by gates, turn left and walk uphill to join a lane. Continue uphill, past a farm and almost at the top, go left over an awkward stile into the Broadway Tower Country Park. Note the warnings about payment should you step an inch off the public footpath, and you'll have to pay if you want to use the picnic area, a huge chess game or the café. Follow the grassy path and climb a ladder stile. Pass left of the Rookery Barn, and follow arrows to go through a metal gate on the left, by the exit. Head for the Tower.

This was built as a folly for the Earl of Coventry in the 18th century. William Morris, the Victorian craftsman and poet, once lived here and a display of his life and work can be seen. For a fee, you can climb to the castellated roof and enjoy the spectacular views, stretching, it is claimed, across 12 counties from the brooding outline of the Black Mountains in Wales to the Berkshire Downs way to the south. So, start counting! Go through a gate to the right of the Tower which, depending on the size of your rucksack or stomach, you may find a bit of a squeeze! Turn left downhill, joining the Cotswold Way for the journey back to Broadway. This magnificent

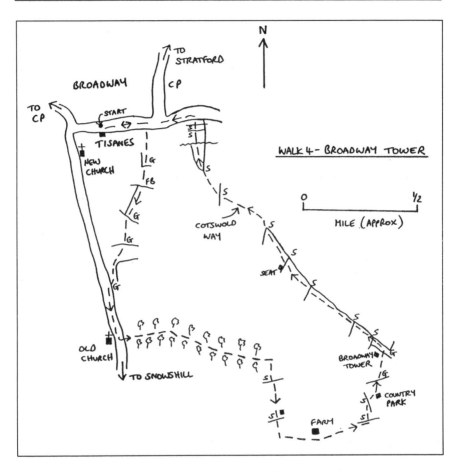

long distance footpath runs from Bath to Chipping Campden through some of the finest countryside in southern England.

Cross one stile and keep the wall on the right over the next three. The horrendous scar ripping across the countryside to the right is the new bypass which, as well as devouring yet more acres, also cuts across what was a marvellous footpath on Fish Hill. Go down steps by a seat, still keeping the wall on the right and cross a stile at the bottom into a field. Follow Cotswold Way signposts downhill, over another stile, and just past the next signpost, bear right to a stile by a gate. The path leads over a brook to another stile by a gate. Cross the stile ahead and go down a lane to the main street where a left turn leads back to Tisanes.

Walk 5. Chaddesley Corbett Woodland

Start/parking: Start in Chaddesley Corbett outside the church, where there is limited street parking, grid reference 892 736.

Distance: 3 or 5 miles.

Summary: A fine walk across farmland returning through glorious woodland. Well waymarked with oodles of mud in the winter and 18 stiles (9 on short route).

Maps: Landranger 139, Pathfinder 953.

Public transport: Daily buses from Bromsgrove and Kidderminster, both of which are served by trains. No Sunday bus service.

The Tea Shop

The Tea Room, High Street, Chaddesley Corbett.

Owned by Jo Powick, whose family also run the Post Office next door, this traditional Tea Room overlooks the half-timbered High Street. Open for three years, it is a popular venue for residents and visitors alike with a cosy atmosphere. Jo does the cooking and two local ladies provide the delicious array of home-made cakes, which include coffee and walnut, fruit cake, iced ginger cake and Victoria sponge. Try the range of sandwiches, cream teas and hot savoury snacks. Prices are low and the portions, including large pots of tea, very generous. When I visited, the Tea Room was being expanded and will seat 30 with patio doors opening onto the rear. Open: 10.00am-5.00pm every day, 2.00pm-6.00pm on Sunday all year except for a winter holiday. Tel: 01562 777257.

The Walk

Chaddesley Corbett is one of the most attractive villages in the county, with black and white half-timbered houses dominated by the church spire. Originally just called Chaddesley, the Corbett was added when a Norman family of that name took over the manor at the end of the 12th century. Later, the land passed to the powerful Beauchamp family.

The church's vast size more befits a town than a village. St Cassian was a Roman schoolmaster stabbed to death by his pupils (must have been those Latin verbs!). The splendid East window, fabulous stonework and an intricately carved Norman font are worth a look. Also inside is a copy, created by a Kidderminster firm, of the 16th century Ardebil carpet, originally woven by a Middle Eastern craftsman. The original, in the Victoria and Albert Museum, took 60 years to complete, was 34 feet long and, is said to contain over 33 million knots. Who counted them?

Follow the lane opposite the church, which bears left in front of a farm, and right past Vicarage Farm. Ignore the first path left and on entering the next large field, turn right alongside a hedge. Just before a gate, climb a stile and turn left. Follow the hedge on the left around the edge of the field. Cross a stile in the corner and pass right of a pond. Cross another stile and keep the hedge on the right to cross a stile. Keep ahead climbing gradually alongside a line of trees over a large field. Cross a driveway and go ahead on a clear path over a

St Cassian's churchyard, Chaddesley Corbett

field. Cross a stile and go along a path between fences. Cross a stile and follow a narrow path at the edge of a wood. Cross a plank bridge to a lane, turn left. If you decide to follow the **shorter route**, continue up the lane ahead, rejoining the longer route at **(**)**.

For the **longer route**, within 20 metres, turn right over another bridge and stile. Keep the hedge on the left and at the end, go over a fence (broken stile) and through trees to cross another stile by a gate. Aim for farm buildings ahead, turn left by a marker post and bear left through the farmyard. Go through a metal gate, following the arrows. Ignore a stile (left) and keep ahead over a stile by a gate. Cross the stile in the hedge ahead. Keep ahead to cross a stile by a power pole onto a minor road. Turn right along the lane and just past Woodcote, turn left along a rough lane by a signpost. Bear left, keeping to the bridleway passing left of a house to go through a gate and alongside woods. Turn left in front of Highwood Cottage and pass through gate at the end into a path between fences. Go through the gate ahead into Nutnells Wood and follow the muddy bridleway through the wood.

Ignore the gate on the left and continue ahead to emerge onto a lane through another gate. Turn left past Randan Cottage and at the next drive by a house called Randan, turn right down the drive. Pass right of the garage and cross a stile into Chaddesley Wood Nature Reserve. In Worcestershire, Chaddesley is second only in size to the Wyre Forest and was once part of the Royal Forest of Feckenham. The Worcestershire Wildlife Trust has recently taken over its management. The wood is a mix of sessile and pedunculate oak, birch, hazel and conifers with a rich understorey of rowan, holly and hawthorn. Wood sorrel forms part of a varied ground flora and alder thrives near the streams. The mixture of trees at varying stages of maturity combined with scrub makes it a valuable habitat for birdlife. Summer visitors include tree pipits and various warblers while crossbills sometimes breed among the conifers. Woodcock, an elusive bird, can be found along the woodland edge on summer evenings.

Follow the clear path ahead along the woodland edge where a breathtaking display of bluebells brightens a spring day. Emerge onto a lane and cross the stile ahead into a field. Keep to the right edge of the field alongside the wood, and at the corner, cross a stile back into Chaddesley Wood. Turn left on a clear path past a conifer plantation and keep ahead past a marker post. Ignore the next path

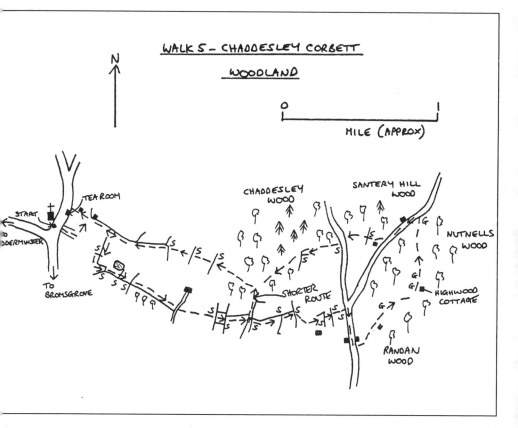

(left), keep ahead to where the path joins another (the Jubilee Trail). Keep ahead and at the next junction, the shorter route comes in from the left (**). Bear right (or **left** from the **shorter route!**) downhill. At the bottom, before a grassy clearing, bear left. Ignore any side paths and cross a stile at the edge of the wood. Follow the clear path under pylons, over another stile and across the field ahead. Cross another stile and follow the hedge on the right to rejoin the outward path. Where the lane bends left, keep ahead past allotments to a lane. Continue ahead, left of a double garage to the main street. The Tea Room is just to the left – perfect timing!

Walk 6. Evesham Abbey and Riverside

Start/parking: Several car parks in Evesham. The one at Merstow Green, just off Vine Street, is the nearest to the Almonry Museum, from where the walk starts, grid reference 035 436.

Distance: 3 or 5 miles.

Summary: A pleasant wander through an historic town, with a rich monastic past, combined with a stroll alongside the river Avon. The shorter route misses out the crossing of the busy bypass. Plenty of mud on the riverside paths and there are 3 stiles (one on the short route).

Maps: Landranger 150, Pathfinder 1020.

Public transport: Regular trains from Hereford, Malvern, Worcester, Oxford and London Paddington. Frequent buses from all directions including London, Worcester, Malvern, Cheltenham, Tewkesbury and Stratford upon Avon.

The Tea Shops

The Mews Coffee Pot, Vine Mews, Evesham.

Almost opposite the Almonry Museum, the Mews Coffee Pot is a cosy, delightful hideaway, with a welcoming ambience away from the noise and traffic of the main street. Inside are pine tables and during the summer, tables outside take advantage of the sun trap courtyard setting. Everything but the paté and bread is home-made by the owner, Wendy Dyde, and the comprehensive specials board changes regularly, always with a choice of at least six substantial dishes. The bacon hotpot is particularly popular, one customer travelling all the way from Bristol for his regular fix! The range of cakes and slices on offer is guaranteed to make addicts like myself break out in a tizzy of indecision. When the mood takes her, Wendy does change some of the cakes, even though her regulars greet the absence of a favourite with dismay. The sausage rolls looked scrumptious or you can have jacket potatoes, cream teas, sandwiches and soups, all reasonably priced. Wendy has recently received a Highly Commended award in the Good Café Guide. Open all year from 10.00am-4.30pm in winter and 10.00am-5.00pm in summer, although Wendy can stay open later if a group books in advance. Just give her a ring! Tel: 01386 49009.

The Gateway, Evesham.

This half-timbered building sits snugly by Abbot Reynald's Gateway, hence the name. The striking gateway was built in the 12th century and retains some of the original arcading. Marcus, Ann and Jackie La Porta took over in 1998 and, as well as providing home-made traditional fare, have found time to refurbish this delightful teashop. Speciality teas are available, along with a tempting choice of light snacks, cakes and sandwiches. Their Gateway Afternoon Tea is very popular and a specials board offers light lunches, along with vegetarian options, between 11.45am and 2.00pm. In summer, you can sit outside, overlooking the churches on one side and the Market Square on the other. Open: 9.30am-5.00pm all week between March and October, and six days a week at other times. Tel: 01386 442249.

The Gateway Tea room

The Walk

The river Severn snakes through Evesham in the shape of a giant
U-bend and the bustling market town at its heart boasts a rich monastic and architectural past. The Abbey was built in the 8th century
by Egwin, Bishop of Worcester and the remaining Bell Tower and
Gateway, as well as the Cloister Arch, only hint at its former glory.
The original Abbey, one of the richest in the country, was close in
size to Gloucester Cathedral. Standing high on a terrace above the
river, it must have dominated the town. The Almonry Museum itself
was once the home of the Abbey's Almoner, who was responsible for
distributing relief to the sick and poor of the town. Nearby was the
Abbey Home Farm with its attendant barns, kitchens, stables and
brewhouses – the monastery and its surrounding buildings formed
an entire community in itself. It did not survive Henry VIII's dissolution.

In the 13th century, the Battle of Evesham ended the Barons' War.
Barely 50 years after the Magna Carta was signed, Simon de
Montfort, Henry III's brother in law, was made leader of a council
aimed at controlling royal power. Civil war was the inevitable con-
clusion as the monarchy resisted the curbs. In August 1265, after
months of bloody fighting, Prince Edward met Simon's army near
the river at Evesham where the Barons' outnumbered army was
slaughtered. Before the battle, Simon prophesied "Now God have
mercy on our souls, for our bodies are our enemies". A memorial to
Simon stands in Abbey Park on the site of his original burial, by the
Abbey's high altar.

From the Almonry, go past the stocks, now presumably used for
argumentative tourists, and turn right into Abbey Park. The information boards in front of the churches of St Lawrence and All
Saints, and scattered about the Park, are a marvellous idea and bring
the image of the vast Abbey and its monastic routine vividly to life.
Continue past the churches and through the Bell Tower archway.
Take the middle (half right) of three paths past the memorial to Simon de Montfort. The cloister arch is away to the right. Walk past
the war memorial and down to the riverside. The pools you pass
were once some of the Abbey fishponds.

Turn right, (river on the left) through the park and under Abbey
bridge. Continue alongside the river on a muddy path, which swings
in a wide loop past the Hampton rope-drawn ferry. Keep alongside

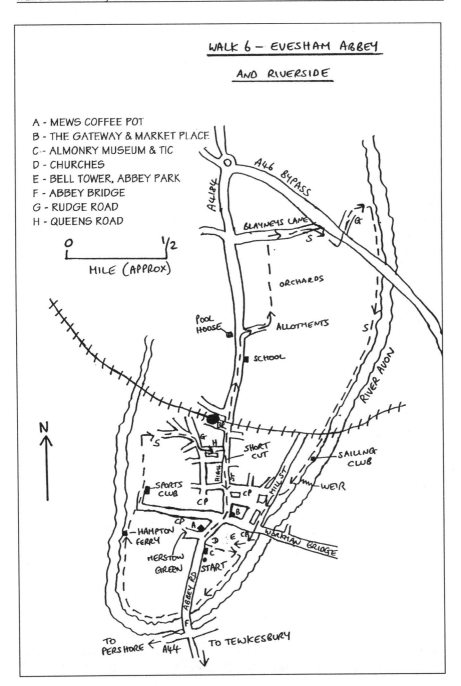

WALK 6 - EVESHAM ABBEY

AND RIVERSIDE

A - MEWS COFFEE POT
B - THE GATEWAY & MARKET PLACE
C - ALMONRY MUSEUM & TIC
D - CHURCHES
E - BELL TOWER, ABBEY PARK
F - ABBEY BRIDGE
G - RUDGE ROAD
H - QUEENS ROAD

0   1/2

MILE (APPROX)

the river to a road. Continue left of the Sports Club and through a gate into rugby fields. Just past the first field, turn right by white railings to cross a stile by a gate. Walk up the narrow path, join a road by an industrial estate and turn right. In 50 metres, turn right across Rudge Road and take the first left, Queens Road. At the main street, you can **shorten** the route by turning right down the High Street to Vine Street. You pass the Market Place where the curiously named Round House stands. Curious because the building couldn't be squarer if it tried!

For the **longer route**, cross the road and turn left to cross the railway bridge. Continue uphill and after half a mile, pass a school. Opposite Pool House, turn right down an alleyway, by a footpath sign, between houses. Emerge by allotments with lovely views stretching across the Vale of Evesham to Meon Hill and the Cotswolds. The Vale lies on incredibly fertile soil, producing a wide range of vegetables and fruit. During spring, it becomes a riot of colour as the apple and plum trees bob under the weight of the blossom. During the 19th century, this industry was of such importance to the Vale that schools would close and farmers employed hundreds of children and their families to pick the fruit. Continue ahead, bearing left at the corner by a marker post and walk along the left edge of an orchard and fields to Blayneys Lane. Turn right downhill and where tarmac swings right, continue ahead on a rough track between bushes. At the end of the track, cross a stile somewhat obscured in the undergrowth. Keep the wire fence, and bypass, on the left to the corner by a lane.

Turn left and, with great care, cross this extremely fast road. Continue ahead down the lane, and after 100 metres, go through a gate on the right, by a yellow arrow. Head half left downhill to the riverside and turn right, (river on the left). Go under the bypass bridge, named after Simon de Montfort. The path continues by the river through several fields negotiating a broken fence, rickety footbridge and oodles of mud before going through a metal kissing gate. Walk through a bush tunnel, and use the wooden boardwalk under the railway bridge. Emerge by the sailing club. Turn left and by a no cycling sign, turn left down an alleyway. Follow the path alongside the fence past the weir to Mill Street. Turn left and at the junction, keep left again. At the end of the road by Workman Bridge, cross and walk down the alleyway to Abbey Park. Follow any path to the right uphill past the Bell Tower to the start.

Walk 7. Great Malvern

Start/parking: As for Walks 13 and 18, start from the railway station, grid reference 784 457. Ample parking in Great Malvern.

Distance: 3½ miles.

Summary: A fascinating circuit of an intriguing town, rich in history, with wide, tree-lined streets and elegant Victorian buildings. As Great Malvern occupies a series of terraces, this walk is surprisingly hilly but there are no stiles.

Maps: OS Explorer 14, Landranger 150. Local shops also stock a large scale (1:10,000) covering the whole Malvern ridge on three maps and a street plan is available from the TIC.

Public transport: Trains from Stratford upon Avon, Hereford, Worcester, Evesham, Oxford, Birmingham and London. Frequent buses from Birmingham, Bromsgrove, Droitwich, Worcester, Cheltenham and Ledbury.

The Tea Shops

Bluebird Tea Room, Church Street, Malvern

Situated above a shoe shop, climbing the stairs to the Bluebird is like entering a quaint, front parlour. Popular with residents and visitors alike, the two low-ceilinged rooms with lace cloths on each table and old prints on the wall, are complemented by cheery service and home cooked food. There has been a tea room here since 1913, although not established, as they point out on the menu, by the current owners, Norman and June Williams! They had a restaurant in Bromyard before running a hotel and restaurant in Pembrokeshire for 11 years. Everything from jacket potatoes, salads and sandwiches to hot snacks are available. Home-made soup, a range of savoury baps and delicious puddings, including a truly scrumptious apple pie, complete an interesting menu. Open Tuesday to Saturday, 9.30am-5.00pm. Tel: 01684 561166.

Lyttelton Well Coffee Shop, Church Street, Great Malvern

Tucked away in a courtyard, the Coffee Shop, opened in 1993 and run by volunteers, as part of a Christian Centre which provides a vital service for the local community. The project offers a counselling service, bookshop and halls which serve as venues for support groups, lunch clubs, a nursery school and fund-raising events. The Coffee Shop menu offers a range of hot snacks between 11.30am and 3.30pm, together with ploughman's and salads. Generous portions of delicious cakes, teacakes, scones and cream teas, all at extremely reasonable prices, are available all day. The atmosphere is welcoming and you can sit at pine tables inside or outside by the symbolic well. Open: Monday to Saturday 10.00am-5.00pm plus Bank Holidays, except Good Friday. Tel: 01684 573702.

The Walk

Great Malvern is set steeply into the lower slopes of the Worcestershire Beacon and on our walk, we shall see a fascinating blend of architecture ranging from Georgian elegance to Gothic grandeur. During Victorian times, Great Malvern became a fashionable spa, which owed much of its subsequent prosperity to the purity of its water. The grand Priory church is almost hemmed in by other buildings and it's only as you climb towards the hills that you can appreciate its sheer size. Few towns can boast such a wealth of literary and musical connections. Edward Elgar spent much of his life in Worcestershire. Born in 1857 at Broadheath, near Worcester, he lived in Malvern for many years and is buried in a simple grave at St Wulstan's church, Little Malvern. His music reflects his deep love of these hills and the surrounding countryside.

From the railway station, turn right and at the junction, turn right over the railway bridge. Cross over and walk past the Girls' College, with rather ostentatious gryphons on the gateposts. This was once the Imperial Hotel, the grandest in the town, which could boast its own underground tunnel to the station, nicknamed the "worm". Just before the church, turn left down an alleyway to Barnard's Green Road. Cross over and turn right. Turn left down Wilton Road to the cemetery. Pass right of the church to see the grave of Jenny Lind, the Swedish Nightingale. She came to Malvern in 1883 and lived at Wynds Point on the hills until her death in 1887. From her grave, pass right of the church again and head for the top (north) corner of the cemetery. From this perspective, the hills form a marvellous

Great Malvern from the path to St Ann's Well

backdrop to the town. Leave via the vehicle entrance, by allotments and turn left along Madresfield Road.

Just after the railway bridge, turn right down Lansdowne Crescent by the Methodist Church. At the junction, turn left past the hospital. These Regency houses are reminiscent of another Lansdowne Crescent in Leamington Spa. Back on Madresfield Road, turn right past Manor Park and continue up Church Street. Turn left down Priory Road (by a parking sign) and go straight over the crossroads. Turn right into Priory Park past the swimming baths entrance. Priory Park was once part of Abbey lands and a spring visit reveals a wealth of colour with pink hawthorn and magnolia blossom, together with many unusual trees. Bear left to cross the bridge over Swan Pool, previously the monks' source of fresh fish. Go past the bandstand to see the newly renovated Winter Gardens complex, containing a theatre, concert hall and cinema. If it's open, you can go up the steps and through the building to Grange Road beyond. If not, pass left of the building to emerge from the park into Grange Road.

Almost opposite the theatre is an alleyway, which leads up to the Priory churchyard. The Lyttelton Well is by the other churchyard

entrance to the right. On the original site of the church was an 11th
century Benedictine priory, which did not survive the dissolution.
The church was bought by locals who paid the then enormous sum
of £20 for it. One of its greatest treasures is a collection of 15th century wall and floor tiles, originally part of the choir screen and floor.
The ones you see today are replicas as the originals are too delicate to
be trampled on. Go up the steps in front of the church, and turn left
through an archway to emerge below Belle Vue Terrace. The Abbey
Gateway, which now houses the Malvern museum, survives from
the original Benedictine monastery, and in the archway you can still
see hinged wooden gateposts. Next to these is the Porter's Squint, a
niche that allowed the gatekeeper to vet approaching visitors.

Cross to the opposite, and highest, part of the road by Lloyds Bank
and turn left. Turn right into Rose Bank Gardens and turn left. Notice the gas lamp on the corner, one of almost a hundred still in use.
You can follow any of the parallel paths through the gardens, which
offer lovely views across the town. The Abbey Hotel, covered in ivy,
and backed by the church tower is a particularly splendid sight.
Halfway through the gardens you can see buildings to the left which
were used for hydrotherapy treatment. The separate buildings for
males and females were connected by a Bridge of Sighs. In the 18th
century, Dr John Wall pronounced the spring water "famous for containing just nothing at all". In 1842, Drs. Wilson and Gully introduced hydrotherapy treatments, which transformed the town. Mind
you, when you read the details of the "cure", you have to admire the
patients' stamina. They were wrapped in wet sheets, then plunged
in a cold bath, before walking to the spring. Other treatments included water being poured from a height onto the shivering patient
below. They probably counted themselves lucky to escape pneumo-
nia. We pass St Ann's Well, the site of one of the springs, on walks 13
and 18.

Leave the gardens at the southern end via an iron gate and continue along the grassy terrace. Where the path dips to road level,
cross over (the next steps don't allow a good view of the traffic) and
turn right. Where the road forks, bear left down Wells Road. Turn
left on the first hairpin into Abbey Road. Turn right down College
Road, which swings downhill, and left to pass Malvern College for
boys, which opened in 1865. At the end, note the unusual Victorian
pillar box on the opposite corner. Turn right and just past the
Lindsay Arts Centre, turn right down an alleyway. Emerge by more

College buildings and a choice of three roads. Go down the middle one, Albert Road South and at the crossroads, turn right down Clarence Road. At the next junction, take the second left, Imperial Road, which leads back to the station.

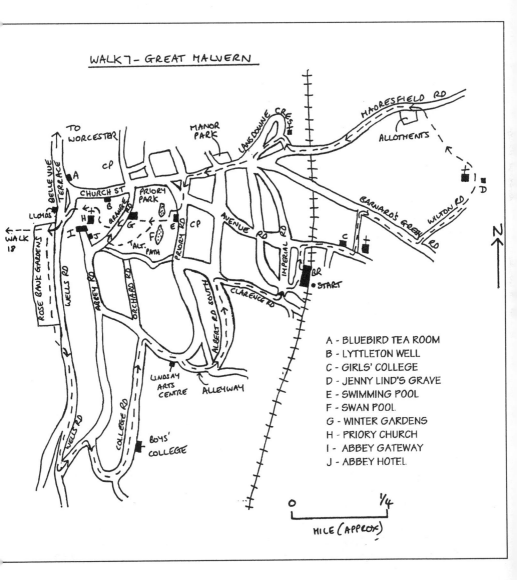

A - BLUEBIRD TEA ROOM
B - LYTTLETON WELL
C - GIRLS' COLLEGE
D - JENNY LIND'S GRAVE
E - SWIMMING POOL
F - SWAN POOL
G - WINTER GARDENS
H - PRIORY CHURCH
I - ABBEY GATEWAY
J - ABBEY HOTEL

Walk 8. Hanbury and Piper's Hill

Start/parking: Jinney Ring Craft Centre, grid reference 963 641. Permission has been given for walkers to park at the centre, using the lower car park, but please check first. When the centre is closed, alternative parking is possible at Pipers Hill wood.

Distance: 6½ miles.

Summary: A fine varied circuit across farmland initially to Piper's Hill wood, climbing to Hanbury churchyard and its superb views before walking through the parkland of Hanbury Hall. The waymarking could be improved and there are 23 stiles, some quite awkward.

Maps: Landranger 150, Pathfinder 974.

Public transport: Only one bus per day from Droitwich. Nearest BR stations at Bromsgrove or Droitwich.

The Tea Shop

The Farmhouse Kitchen, Jinney Ring Craft Centre, Hanbury.

The Jinney Ring Craft Centre was established by Richard and Jenny Greatwood in restored barns 19 years ago. During that time, the centre has won awards for outstanding new tourist enterprise and for the sensitive conversion of the buildings. Craftsmen in leather, needlework, stained glass, jewellery, pottery, clothing, painting and antiques are just some whose workshops you can visit. The craft gallery holds a range of exhibitions through the year and courses are run to give you the opportunity to learn a new skill.

The Farmhouse Kitchen is an extremely popular part of the Centre. From the time they opened, a tea shop was always available but around 13 years ago, Richard "moved" a barn from the village and spent two years restoring it. This airy, timbered building is an ideal setting for a restaurant where home cooking is the watchword. A superb choice of lunches is available between 12.00noon-2.00pm including soup, lasagne, hot pots and quiches. Served all day is an equally delicious range of cakes, sweets and teas, with banoffee pie a particular favourite.   Tables on the grass outside overlook a duckpond with views to the Malverns beyond. Open all year from Tuesday to Saturday 10.30am-5.00pm and 11.30am-5.30pm on Sundays. Admission is free. Tel: 01527 821653.

The Walk

The village of Hanbury is scattered either side of an old Roman road, now used by the modern Droitwich to Alcester highway. The village school and church are some distance from the main community and, in the case of the church, perched high on a hilltop. From the Craft Centre, turn right down the road to almost opposite Woodrow Farm. Go left through a gate onto a footpath. Keep the hedge on the left, past a coppice of trees and a reservoir. Go through a gate onto the road and turn left. At the next corner, keep ahead on a bridleway for a mile to another road. Turn left and where the road goes left, keep ahead past a signpost and over a stile into a field.

Keep the fence on the right to go through a gate in the top corner. Skirt right of the farm, noting the unusual barn used as a dovecote. Go through a gate and ahead up the lane to Piper's Hill wood, now in the care of the Worcestershire Wildlife Trust. Such a wood, predominantly magnificent beeches, is unusual in the Midlands and reminds me, on a smaller scale of my old stomping ground, Burnham Beeches, in the Chilterns. A scattering of other trees includes sweet

St Mary the Virgin church, Hanbury

chestnut and oaks, which provide the holes and cavities so valuable to nesting little and tawny owls, nuthatches and all three species of woodpeckers. Cross the cattle grid and turn right. Where the track bends right, keep ahead inside the edge of the wood.

Cross the road and bear left through the car park. Walk downhill, with a pond to the right and follow a path along the edge of the woods. At the top corner, emerge onto a farm track. Aim for the kissing gate ahead, and go past a pond, through another gate and uphill to St Mary's church. This is featured in the "Archers" BBC radio serial and many of the characters were "married" here. From the road in front of the church, go downhill and just past the Coach House, turn right and go through a gate into the parkland of Hanbury Hall. The path heads downhill aiming for a gap in the trees ahead. Cross the stile and bear half right along an avenue of trees. Cross the stile by a yellow topped post, and after 100 metres, go over an awkward stile on the left. Turn right alongside the fence and where this bends right, keep ahead over the open field.

Just over the rising ground, cross a stile by an iron gate. Pass a pond, keep ahead and when the ground rises, aim for two stone memorials. From here, bear slightly left (at 11 o'clock) and head for the far fence. The odd marker post in this vast expanse wouldn't come amiss. As you can see from the map, other footpaths cross this area but there's no clue on the ground. Reach a stile by a pond, and although there's no arrow for this direction, cross the stile and turn left. Keep the fence and then woodland on the left over two stiles. Cross another two awkward stiles by a ditch. After 100 metres, cross a stile on the left by a house. Walk past a pond, cross another awkward stile to the road and then the stile left into Hanbury Hall parkland. Head for the church on the skyline (again, a marker post to indicate the direction would help). As you near a solitary spreading cedar, bear left to cross a stile in the fence by the wall surrounding Hanbury Hall.

Pass the entrance to the Hall, undeniably impressive and with many elegant features. I doubt if they would welcome walkers in muddy boots inside but the grounds are worth visiting, particularly the ice house and Orangery. The Hall, cared for by the National Trust, is open from April to October, Saturdays to Wednesdays in the afternoons. Cross the drive and stile ahead. Walk under the power line and bear half right to cross a stile in the fence. Cross the road and go through the gate opposite, with the house to the left.

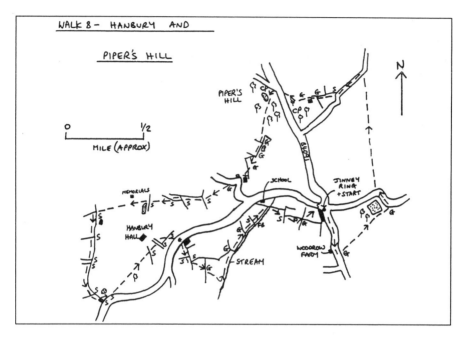

This next mile has, at the time of writing, no waymarks and some awkward stiles. Keep the fence on the left to cross a stile in the top corner. Turn left and immediately cross another stile (if 4 wobbly planks of wood can be called a stile) into the next field. Head diagonally right to go through a broken gate halfway along the opposite hedge.

From here the path heads to the top right corner of the field, then doubles back left alongside a stream by the hedge opposite. In effect, you are aiming for a gate in the top left corner of this field. Go through the gate and keep the stream on the right. Go through the next gate (after puzzling how anyone fatter than a stick insect is supposed to climb the stile by the tree). Keep the hedge on the right to go over a stile, then cross a plank bridge by a pond. Almost at the end of the hedge, turn right along a well defined path (school to the left). Follow the path to cross a stile and keep ahead. Just past a pond, bear left to go through a gate. In the next field, head half right to a stile in the hedge. Cross two stiles onto the road and turn right to a junction by the Craft Centre.

Walk 9. Holt Heath and Ombersley

Start/parking: Permission has been given to park at Bramleys Tea Shop, just
                       off the A4133, Holt Heath, grid reference 821 632, but please
                       check first and bear in mind the closing time of 4.30.
                       Alternative parking is possible in the main street at Ombersley.

Distance: 6 miles.

Summary: A delightful walk alongside the River Severn on the Wychavon
                       Way and through woodland and parkland to the lovely village
                       of Ombersley. A return across mixed farmland with extensive
                       views adds variety to a walk which sometimes throws up
                       eccentric waymarking. 12 stiles.

Maps: Landranger 138, Pathfinder 974.

Public transport: Buses to Holt Heath and Ombersley from Worcester and
                       Kidderminster via Stourport or Hartlebury. Also from Tenbury
                       Wells as far as Holt Heath. No Sunday service. Nearest BR
                       stations at Droitwich and Hartlebury.

The Tea Shop

Bramleys, Holt Heath.

Bramleys, situated within the farm shop at Broomfields Farm, is run
by Wendy Coles. Her son in law, Colin, and daughter, Fiona, run the
farm, which has a history dating back to 1910. The superb farm shop
sells 30 varieties of their own apples and pears, together with a large
range of other locally produced vegetables and fruit, as well as tradi-
tionally produced preserves. A mini garden centre also provides an
excellent choice of plants and shrubs.

Opened in December 1996, Bramleys offers home-made food from
a variety of sources. The majority is made on the premises by Wendy
and you can see her slaving away in the adjacent kitchen. The menu,
which includes vegetarian choices, is changed periodically and a
specials board offers a variety of new recipes. You can enjoy soup,
baked potatoes, toasted snacks, quiche and salad, as well as more
substantial dishes such as casseroles, pies and pasta. Sample the
mouth-watering range of desserts including sticky toffee pudding,

apple pie and the sinful chocolate bread and butter pudding. Tea cakes, scones, and an array of cakes can be washed down with an interesting range of tea and coffee. During the summer, you can sit outside and in winter, a wood burning stove provides welcome heat as well as complementing the timbered ceiling and flagstone floor. A selection of magazines and toys is a nice touch. Open every day from 10.00am-4.30pm, closed at Xmas and New Year. Tel: 01905 621840.

The Walk

From Bramleys, return to the main road, and turn left to cross the bridge over the River Severn. At the far side, go left down steps and turn left under the bridge to join the Wychavon Way, at the start of its journey to Winchcombe. Follow the riverside path over two stiles to pass right of a pub. Walk through the next two fields, (three stiles) with an impressive wooded escarpment to the left. At the end of the third field, cross two more stiles by a bridge over a stream. Halfway along the next field is an obscure marker post by the riverbank. Turn left up a raised tongue of land to cross a stile into a wood, still on the Wychavon Way.

Ombersley

The muddy path climbs through trees to a rough lane, which bends left in front of a gate. Ignore the stile on the right (where the eccentric waymarking begins), and follow the lane to a large pond. Turn left across the end of it and at the next bend, turn right by a marker post (accurate this time). Walk along the left edge of the pond to a large reed bed, home to birds such as reed buntings, sedge and reed warblers. The path eventually bears left away from the pond into a field. Turn right along the field edge and at an overgrown corner, emerge into the next field. Head half right, parallel to the tree line on the right. The towering spire of the church and the grim frontage of Ombersley Court can be seen away to the left. At the end of the field, cross the stile but ignore the potty waymark (pointing the wrong way – from whichever direction you arrive!). Continue ahead across parkland, right of a wooden enclosure and through a gate to the road.

Turn left through Ombersley, a village of beauty and distinction, full of black and white, timber framed houses. Inside the lofty St Andrew's are some of the original box pews, including a manorial pew complete with fireplace and curtain rails. In the early 1800s, the church became unstable and while the authorities were debating the need for repairs, arguments were cut short when the whole lot fell down. Thomas Rickman designed the new church which, we hope, was built on firmer foundations in the 1820s.

When you reach the roundabout, look for an unusual, hollowed-out plague stone on the green. This was originally on the old packhorse road, west of the Court, and during the time of the Black Death it served as a warning to travellers to avoid the village (presumably, like the plague!). It also acted as a place where provisions could be left for the villagers. Turn left at the roundabout, cross the road and turn right down Apple Tree Walk. Take the first left and at the end, turn right past houses. At the end, continue ahead on a surfaced footpath, which passes a water tower to reach Uphampton. Turn left along the lane, which soon bends right to a T-junction by Corner Cottage. Turn left and where the view opens out, (just past a footpath sign left), turn right down a rough lane (no signpost). Ignore the stile (right) and keep the hedge on the left down the field.

The clocktower and hills ahead belong to Abberley. Halfway down the field, the path switches fields and continues with the hedge on the right (on a different line from the Pathfinder). Views here encompass the Malverns to the left and Shrawley Wood on the right. The path reaches a lane, where you turn right past Boreley House. Take the footpath on the left, which heads half right across the field to a footpath sign and steps which can be overgrown in summer. Turn left along the lane and where this bends left, continue ahead passing left of the buildings to go down a tarmac lane. This goes past Mutton Hall caravan park and just before another bend, turn left over a stile and head for the riverside. Lenchford Inn, on the opposite bank, is out of reach of even the thirstiest walker (unless you can bribe a passing boat). Turn left and follow the riverside path through fields, crossing two stiles to pass Holt Lock. Follow the lane to Holt Fleet bridge where you turn right back to the start.

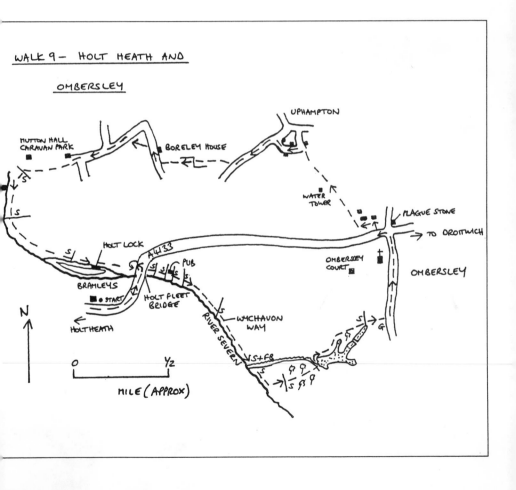

Walk 10. Kyre Park and Hanley Child

Start/parking: Permission has been given to use the car park at Kyre
(pronounced Keer) Park Gardens, when they are open, grid
reference 626 636, but please check first. When these are
closed, alternative parking is possible at Stoke Bliss Village
Hall picnic place, half a mile away at grid reference 630 632,
joining the walk at point **.

Distance: 5½ miles.

Summary: A lovely, varied circuit featuring woodland, orchards, churches,
glorious views and a beautiful garden. The route is surprisingly
hilly, with plenty of mud and 7 stiles, along with one slippery
descent to cross a stream. Waymarking is generally adequate
with just a few blank spots.

Maps: Landranger 138 or 149, Pathfinder 973.

Public transport: Limited daily service (not Sundays) from Hereford and Tenbury
Wells to Kyre stopping on the B4214.

The Tea Shop

Tea Room, Kyre Park Gardens

Occupying an annexe to Kyre Park House and adjacent to the
church, it would be hard to imagine a more delightful, tranquil setting for a Tea Room. There are tables inside the spacious interior,
while others outside overlook a lawn and a lake bedecked with lilies.
After a walk, it's hard to beat sitting with a pot of tea and a wedge of
something gooey watching the house martins buzzing overhead. A
selection of dishes offers everything from a quick snack of both "ordinary" and toasted sandwiches to light lunches of jacket potatoes,
soup and ploughman's, all with different fillings. Equally tempting
is a range of home-baked cakes and delicious desserts. The service is
prompt and friendly and the prices reasonable. Open daily
11.00am-6.00pm, currently from Easter to the end of the year. Tel:
01885 410247.

View from Kyre House Gardens pool to Kyre House & its Tea Room, with St Mary's church in the background

The Walk

Tucked away in a remote corner of north west Worcestershire is an area of wooded valleys, orchards, scattered hamlets and rolling hills where the scenery is more reminiscent of neighbouring Herefordshire. Tenbury Wells is the nearest town of any size and the route from any direction is a winding but delightful journey through countryside untainted by modern development. The current Kyre Park House, which is not open to the public, is built around the shell of a Norman castle. After passing through the hands of various families, when the last direct descendant died in 1930, the land was sold and the house gutted. Lord Clarendon, a former High Commissioner for South Africa, began restoration but war intervened and the house was used as a convalescent hospital. It later became a children's TB sanatorium, then a home for adults with cerebral palsy and is now back in private hands. St Mary's Norman church has close links with Kyre Park House – literally, as it's attached to the main part of the house by a covered walkway, in essence, its own cloister.

It's possible to visit the Tea Room, and nursery without going into the gardens, but that would mean missing a treat. Kyre Park Gardens, currently undergoing restoration, are an enchanting jumble of lakes, waterfalls, hermitage ruins, a summer house, shrubs and mature trees in a magic grotto, with a surprise around every corner. By the car park is a Norman dovecote and a tithe barn. Kyre Park is also home to the nursery of Rickards Hardy Ferns, one of the largest award winning collections in the world. The gardens are open daily 11.00-6.00 from Easter to the end of October.

From the second car park by the dovecote, go over the stile in the fence, by the Fern Nursery, and turn left. Keep the fence on the left, through a gateway and continue ahead alongside trees, then a hedge on the left. In the top left corner, continue ahead into another field, with the hedge now on the right. Go over a stile in the top right corner. In 50 metres, before a huge mound, turn right to go through a metal handgate onto the B4214. Turn right and continue, with care, for a quarter of a mile and at a corner by houses, turn left onto a bridleway, signed to Hanley Child. Climb between plantations, ignore a lane to the left and continue between fields and past a barn. Continue between more trees to reach Kyre Pool, an enchanting spot, nestling in a wooded valley and one of the few examples where the hand of man has created something to treasure. This pool, now protected as a nature reserve, was built as a fish pond for Kyre Park House in 1584. In areas of farmland, any sizeable stretch of water proves invaluable to wildlife. We were rewarded with the electric blue flash of a kingfisher darting past. The frantic blacksmith noise you can hear is a hydraulic ram used to pump water.

Go past the pool and through a gate ahead. Turn right up a bank and continue along the edge of the field, with trees to the right. At the end, by a marker post, turn right down the bank to a wide path. Turn left and at the bend, ignore the footpath and bear right. In 50 metres, go left past a bridleway marker and wallow through mud to a gateway. Go through and head half left through the orchard, passing left of a house. Go through a gate, left of a cattle grid and walk ahead, parallel to the drive on the right. When you near the next house, bear left to the top left corner of the field and go through a gate onto a rough lane. Continue ahead along the lane, over a cattle grid and bear left uphill past a house. As you climb, extensive views open out as far as the Clee Hills in Shropshire. At a T-junction, turn right along the lane and left at the next junction to the hamlet of Hanley

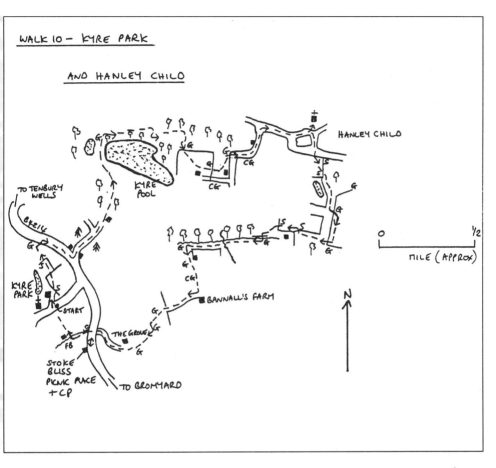

Child. The simple chapel of St Michael and All Angels lies to the left at the end of a grassy path and overlooks the countryside towards the Teme Valley.

Continue along the road, and bear right at the next junction uphill to a T-junction. Cross the stile opposite and head half left across the orchard. Cross another stile and turn right along a wide track, which drops downhill. Go past a large pool (to the right) and ignore the first gate on the left. The path (which could do with a few arrows at this point) now goes ahead between two fences and turns left through the next gate. Turn right alongside the fence uphill to the top right corner of this vast field. Turn right through the gate, and continue ahead. Ignore the path to the left and by the next gate before a house, turn right over a stile. Follow the tree line on the left to cross a stile in the bottom left corner. Turn right along a wide path (ignore the footbridge left). Don't go through the next metal gate, but turn left through a handgate into a field. Turn right along the edge, parallel to the stream and trees on the right. Ignore the footpath on the right and at the end of the field, follow the track into the wood. This drops steeply on a very slippery path to cross a stream (although this is a bridleway, I shouldn't care to take a horse this way). Climb up the bank to a field. Continue along the woodland edge to the top right corner, then walk between a fence (left) and trees (right) to go through a handgate onto a wide track.

Turn left past houses and through another gate to a drive. Keep ahead along the rough lane, which bears right and crosses a cattle grid. Just before Bannall's Farm, turn right through a gate and along the left edge of the field. The wooded tangle on the left is an overgrown moat, built around an earlier house. Follow the hedge on the left to the bottom corner and go straight through a gap into the next field. Head straight across the next field and through a gate in the tree line. Keep ahead, with the hedge on the left to the corner and turn left through a handgate. Head half right across the field and after a rise in the ground, aim for a gap in the tree line ahead. Join a wide, muddy track and bear left through a gateway. Keep the hedge on the right to a lane by The Grove farm. Follow this to the B4214, where the alternative parking at Stoke Bliss picnic place is to the left (**). Cross the stile opposite into an orchard. Walk ahead, stream on the right and turn right over a footbridge. Go ahead, passing right of a house to reach a stony lane back to Kyre Park Gardens.

Walk 11. Lickey Hills and Bittell Reservoirs

Start/parking: Visitor Centre, Lickey where there is ample parking, grid reference 998 756.

Distance: 4½ miles

Summary: A surprisingly varied hilly circuit on the fringe of Birmingham. Magnificent woodland, extensive views, bracing reservoirs and a minute church all feature on this well waymarked walk. Plenty of mud is on offer and there are 10 stiles.

Maps: Landranger 139, Pathfinders 953 and 954.

Public transport: British Rail station at Barnt Green on route of walk with trains from Lichfield, Birmingham and Redditch. Buses to Barnt Green and Cofton Hackett from Birmingham, Bromsgrove and Halesowen but no Sunday service. Between May and September on Sundays and Bank Holidays only, a "walkers'" bus from Barnt Green visits Lickey on a round trip to Kidderminster which includes Waseley, Clent and Kinver.

The Tea Shop

Café, Visitor Centre, Lickey Hills Country Park

Lynn Round took over the café here and at Waseley (which we visit on Walk 23) several years ago. A similar menu is on offer in both places, including a substantial all day breakfast and various hot snacks including jacket potatoes, toasted sandwiches, pasties and sausages rolls. These, together with a mug of home-made soup followed by apple pie and custard will keep out the chill on the coldest days. The cakes are particularly popular, all home-made by Lynn. You can choose between tables inside and out, depending on the weather, the service is prompt and friendly and the prices are very reasonable. Open every day from 10.00am-4.30pm in winter and until 7.00pm in summer. Tel: Rangers office 0121 447 7106. Café mobile 0411 430881.

St Michael's church, Cofton Hackett

The Walk

Because of their proximity to Birmingham, the Lickey Hills are a favourite playground for much of the West Midlands population. In fact, on summer weekends it can seem as if everyone of them is here. The area comprises mixed woodland, fragile heathland, bog and an arboretum. Regular coppicing allows sunlight to reach the woodland floor, its warmth giving life to long dormant seeds of bluebells, wood sorrel, foxglove, and dogs mercury. Not least of its treasures is the wide variety of wildlife.

Birds such as jays, treecreepers, great spotted and green woodpeckers abound. Breeding birds such as redstart, redpoll and tree pipit are unusual finds so close to an urban area. During the winter, these woods provide a valuable refuge for flocks of tits and finches with many birds relying on the conifer plantations to survive. In 1997, the entire country witnessed an invasion of crossbills from Scandinavia following failure of the seed crop, their main food. At one point, the conifers by the car park held almost 200 of these striking birds. They utter a distinctive "chip" call, and the other clue to their presence is the pine cones, which threaten to brain you if you stand underneath a feeding flock.

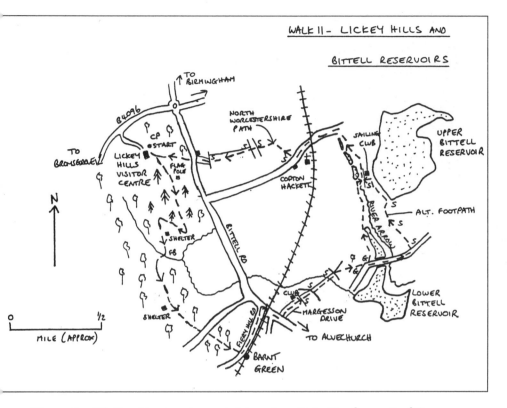

From the Visitor Centre, turn right and walk to the far end of the car park before the track curves left. Turn half right past a wooden barrier to a path under the shade of pine trees. Ignore any side paths and continue on this wide track past seats. At the flagpole, more seats overlook a wonderful viewpoint where you can appreciate your altitude of 600 metres already. You can also trace our route past Bittell Reservoirs. Clever dicks will soon realise that if we're walking all the way down there, it follows that we have to climb all the way back up again. You have been warned! Continue on the main path, which loses height gradually. When the path starts to bear left, by a seat, turn right down steps on a path which winds down through trees. Emerge onto a wide path and turn right past a blue/yellow marker post.

When you reach an even wider stony path, turn left past a horseshoe marker. Go past a wooden shelter and at the bottom of the slope, bear right past (not over) a footbridge. Ignore any side paths and continue uphill, past marker no. 8. The path levels out and passes left of another shelter to reach a lane. Cross to the footpath opposite and walk through the avenue of trees to Barnt Green railway station. Turn left along Fiery Hill Road, parallel to the railway. At a T-junction with Bittell Road, cross and turn right under the railway bridge. Take the first left, Margesson Drive, and at the end, go through the fence gap ahead to a Sports Club (sign to Bittell Farm Road). Pass right of the buildings, and behind the last building, cross a stile into a playing field. Follow the left edge, passing a picnic area and cross a stile. Keep the hedge on the left to the top corner, cross a stile and follow a clear path, right of trees, to the far corner. Go through the gate onto the road.

Here there are two options: either take the bridleway immediately left or a footpath further along the busy road. **For the footpath**, keep ahead along the road crossing a bridge over the Lower Bittell Reservoir. After a quarter of a mile, take the footpath on the lef,twhich crosses a couple of fields between fence and hedge before dropping down to a field corner. Cross a stile, and turn left along the dam of Upper Bittell Reservoir. Turn left again before the Sailing Club to cross a stile by a gate, and turn right along a lane by a pond. **To take the bridleway**, turn left through a gate and follow this wide track with glimpses of the reservoir. The track eventually swings right past a pond to a stile by a gate (where the above alternative emerges).

Continue on the lane, which soon joins tarmac by the Club. Keep ahead and at a T-junction, turn left to go under the railway bridge. In a few metres, go left up steps to the churchyard of St Michael's church, Cofton Hackett (a name which always sounds like a bronchial complaint!). This peaceful spot is surrounded by trees and unusually, the tower still retains its bells. Rejoin the lane and turn left. Just before the next house, turn right over a stile onto the North Worcestershire Path. Keep the hedge on the right and at the end of the field by a marker post, turn left to cross the stile ahead. Nip across the tarmac cycleway, cross the next stile and keep the fence on the right over a long field. Views open out left as far as Brailes Hill (topped with a clump of trees), and Ilmington Hill (two aerials on the summit) in Warwickshire. Aim for the houses ahead, cross a stile in the fence and walk along the alleyway and up the drive to the road. Cross to the path opposite and climb up the path and steps ahead to a broad path. Turn right (still on N.W. Path), and follow the path as it climbs steadily back to the car park.

Walk 12. Madresfield and the Old Hills

Start/parking: Northernmost car park of the Old Hills, just off the western side of the B4424, south of Powick, grid reference 829 487.

Distance: 6½ miles.

Summary: A long, varied circuit across parkland, fields and through woodland with glimpses of the river Severn. Several footpaths can become choked with summer growth, making the walk seem longer than it really is. Some mud in winter, some road walking and 18 stiles.

Maps: Landranger 150, Explorer 14.

Public transport: Buses from Great Malvern and Worcester pass the Old Hills (B4424 road). No Sunday service. Nearest BR stations at Great Malvern and Worcester. One bus from Great Malvern to Madresfield on Fridays.

The Tea Shop

Humphrey's, Madresfield Garden Centre

Inside the garden centre is the deservedly popular Humphrey's Coffee Shop. A neat and spotlessly clean interior is supplemented by courtyard tables overlooked by a magnificent wisteria. Humphrey's occupies the restored former tool shed and apple store. This whole site, originally Madresfield Court's walled garden, has a fascinating history. Hilary Collins and her family took over the site 12 years ago, and five years ago opened the coffee shop. As well as a nursery and retail garden centre, they offer a garden design and build service.

A wide range of goodies is on offer on the imaginative menu, which includes sandwiches, jacket potatoes, toasted pittas and omelettes, supplemented by daily specials. In the summer, a salad bar is very popular and the home-made soups and cakes are very tempting. A busy lunchtime trade includes customers from Malvern businesses. Open all year, every day 10.30am-4.30pm with last orders around 4.00pm in winter. Garden Centre open 9.00am-5.30pm Mon to Sat and 10.00am-5.00pm on Sun. Tel: 01684 574066.

Madresfield Court

The Walk

The Old Hills Common, in the care of the Malvern Hills Conservators and popular with locals, is easy to miss but well worth finding. Bordering both sides of the road, the tangle of scrub and trees is dotted with seats offering views to the Malvern range and Worcester. Winter sunsets seen from here are stunning. Birdlife takes advantage of this haven amid farmland and blackcaps, garden warblers and lesser whitethroats can be found in the hedgerows while butterflies dance along the wide, grassy paths.

With your back to the car park entrance, head for the top right corner of the field. Follow a wide path uphill to pass right of a triangulation point. Head downhill on a wide grass path. Ignore the left fork and at the bottom, continue ahead through bushes and a muddy gateway to a bridleway. In 50 metres, go left over two stiles and head half left over the field. Cross a stile into New Coppice Wood and follow the path through it, crossing an open ride to reach the far side. Cross another stile and turn right to immediately climb another stile by a gate. Turn left, alongside the tree line, with a stream hidden in the ditch. At the end of the field, go through another gate and turn

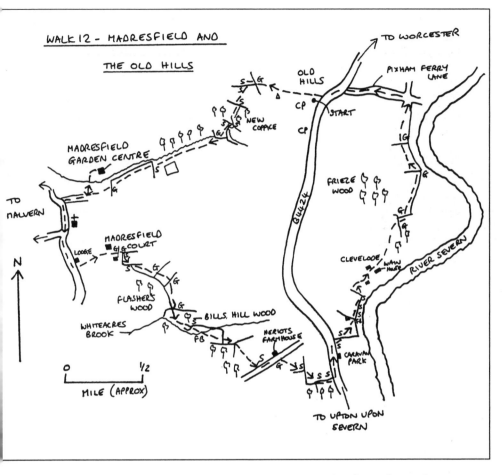

right. Keep the trees and stream on the right until (after a fenced section) you can cross a stile by a gate.

Walk parallel with the fence (right) to the far side of the field. Don't take the stile in the right corner but go through a kissing gate 50 metres further left. Bear right on the estate road, under two bridges and at the next junction, by a grass triangle, turn right. You can follow this lane to the Madresfield Garden Centre by kind permission of Hilary. After filling your face, slosh your way back to the junction, and turn right along the lane to Madresfield village. At the main road, turn left, passing St Mary's church with its unusual well, complete with wrought-iron grill and hoist. Continue south along the road (no pavement) and by a striking half-timbered Lodge (and footpath sign), turn left down the drive.

Ignore the left turn to Madresfield Court and continue ahead, past a striking view of the Court. Although not open to the public, the gardens, renowned for their display of daffodils, are occasionally open during spring and for an Agricultural Show in summer. Go through the gate directly ahead by Home Farm and walk past the magnificent dovecote at the end. Go through the metal gate ahead and turn right over the stile. Keep the buildings to the right and cross the field to go over another stile. Join the muddy track ahead which swings left away from the farm, alongside the fence and Flasher's Wood (you can make up your own jokes for this one)! Follow the arrows for nearly a mile, through two gates and where the track swings left, bear right to the hedge. Ignore the first gate, but go through the second arrowed gate in the corner into Bills Hill Wood. Follow the wide track through the wood with Whiteacres Brook on the right.

At the edge of the wood, by an arrow on a tree, leave the wood and go ahead into a field. On my visit, this next bit was very overgrown with nettles, so gird your loins. Walk ahead for 50 metres, go over a hidden stile on the right and (if it's summer) beat your way over the footbridge. In the field, turn left, parallel to the stream. (There was no sign of a path, so we used the remains of a tractor track through the bean crop – not very comfortable, but passable). At the top of the field, turn right along the hedge and, 50 metres short of the corner by a wood, go left through a gap into the next field. Turn right alongside the hedge and in the corner, turn left along the field edge, parallel to the wood. At the end of the wood, bear half right across the field (use the tractor marks again if necessary), to a stile by a gate just left of the woodland edge. Turn left along the road and just past Heriots Farmhouse, go through a metal gate on the right by a sign. Head half left under power lines and pylons to cross a stile by a gate.

Although the path should go half right, a decent headland had been left along the right edge of the field, turning left at the corner, parallel to a wood. At the edge of the wood, turn right over a stile by a gate. Turn left along the fence to cross a stile by a gate onto the road. Turn left along this busy road past the Riverside Caravan Park and by a footpath sign, turn right over a stile into a field. Head half left to cross another stile. Bear half right to the top right corner of the field by horse barns. Cross the hidden footbridge and stile and turn right on a narrow path between fields and a hedge. Continue on the path with occasional glimpses of the river Severn below on the right. Cross three stiles to Clevelode hamlet.

Turn left along the stony lane to a minor road and turn right. Ignore the footpath, but 20 metres further on, turn left up a tarmac lane (bridleway) past Clevelode Farm. Continue up the lane and by the Wainhouse, ignore the footpath (left), and walk ahead on a grassy lane between fields. The path eventually drops downhill alongside trees to go through a gate. Cross the flood embankment ahead and bear left to go through another gate by a pylon. Head for the top right corner of the field, go through another gate and walk along the stony track. Go through another gate, keep the hedge on the right to join a tarmac lane. This reaches Pixham Ferry Lane, where a left turn and a half mile stretch of uphill walking leads to the car park.

Walk 13. Malvern Railway and Pinnacle Hill

Start/parking: Start from outside the main BR station off Avenue Road, Great Malvern, as for walks 7 and 18, grid reference 784 457.

Distance: 5½ or 6½ miles for the longer option.

Summary: Terrific linear walk starting with a five minute train ride to Colwall, just over the border in Herefordshire. We return to Worcestershire over Pinnacle Hill on the Malverns, with an option to join Walk 18. Glorious views, wooded farmland and plenty of wildlife are highlights of a walk which is all on good footpaths. Waymarking is excellent, there is some mud, considerable climbing but only 3 stiles.

Maps: Explorer 14, Landranger 150. Local shops also stock a large scale (1:10,000) covering the whole ridge in three maps.

Public transport: Same as for Walk 7.

The Tea Shop

Lady Foley's Tea Room, Railway Station, Great Malvern.

Lady Foley's Tea Room occupies part of the Victorian railway station. This atmospheric wooden panelled room is full of character and cheered by a roaring fire in winter. In warmer weather, customers can sit outside at tables on the platform and watch the trains go by. Margaret Baddeley has been here 13 years, initially serving teas and snacks. When the station was destroyed by fire in 1986, Margaret continued to operate from a portacabin. The menu offers everything from a quick snack to a substantial meal including home-made soup, baked potatoes and toasted sandwiches, complemented by salads and quiches. A mouth-watering choice of crumpets, teacakes and scones can round off the day nicely. The menu is changed daily and a take-away service is available. Open all year, Monday to Saturday 9.00am-6.00pm and Sunday 3.00pm-6.00pm. Tel: 01684 893033.

Lady Emily Foley, daughter of the Duke of Montrose, married Edward Foley of Stoke Edith Park in 1832. As Lady of the Manor, she was responsible for much of the planning and layout of the town, resulting in large gardens and houses. She travelled by carriage to the station, where she waited in her own furnished room, now the tea shop.

Lady Foley's Tea Room

The Walk

The railway reached Great Malvern in 1860, the branch line to Upton upon Severn and Tewkesbury opening two years later. After the 1986 fire, the station was carefully restored to its original Victorian splendour. Take a look at the columns supporting the platform roof; each has an individually painted floral pattern. Relax on the one-stop train ride to Colwall because your legs and lungs will soon be working hard! The train passes through Pinnacle Hill via a tunnel around 1500 metres long, which opened in 1926 after the original 19th century tunnel became unsafe.

Leave Colwall station, turn left and cross the railway footbridge past a Worcestershire Way signpost. Drop to a wide track and bear left past a pond. Don't go through the large gate but ahead through a

handgate into a field. Ignore the path to the right and follow the clear
path up the left edge of the field. Your objective, Pinnacle Hill, can
be seen ahead and the only way is up! Cross a stile in the top corner
by a three-way signpost and follow the W. Way South sign ahead up
a grassy bank to a terrace. Bear right past a marker to a wide path. Ignore paths left and right, cross straight over and bear right to climb a
clear path into a large field. After 100 metres, bear left past a marker
post and continue climbing.

Away to the right is the British Camp on Herefordshire Beacon
which looks isolated and hardly part of the main Malvern ridge at
all. At the top of the field, cross a stile and continue up an enclosed
path, then bear right past a marker, with trees on the left. The path
goes through an area of scrub to cross a stile. Now leave the W. Way
and turn left through trees to emerge by a building. Turn right across
open ground, past a car park to cross two roads to another car park by
Gardiners Quarry. At the far right-hand end, join a wide path ahead,
parallel to the road. Go past a "No wheeled vehicles" sign – usually
the cue for cyclists, who wilfully ignore such signs, to come hurtling
round the next corner!

The path climbs gradually, with trees on the left, enjoying lovely
views across Herefordshire. Where the path forks, by a seat, keep
left, climbing to the open hillside between two hills. A few steps further forward, you will see wonderful views east to the Cotswolds. As
we are fairly close to Wales, ravens are quite common. These incredibly acrobatic birds give vent to a wide range of grunts and croaks as
well as their familiar "cronking" call. We were treated to the tremendous spectacle of squadrons of house martins and swallows swoop-
ing and diving all around us. As the Malvern ridge is a prominent
landmark, it's a good spot during spring and autumn to witness such
large scale bird movements.

Turn left, keeping to the highest part of the ridge, over another hill
before reaching Pinnacle Hill, at just over a thousand feet. The circular depressions on the summit are the excavated remains of Bronze
Age burial chambers. Continue along the ridge, dropping downhill
to pass right of a conifer plantation. Go round or over the next two
hills, after which all paths converge at the end of the ridge to join a
repaired path down to Wyche Cutting, believed to be named after an
ancient saltway. Cross the busy road, with care, and turn right up
Beacon Road (there's usually an ice cream van here in the summer –
another of my weaknesses!). Continue uphill through the car park

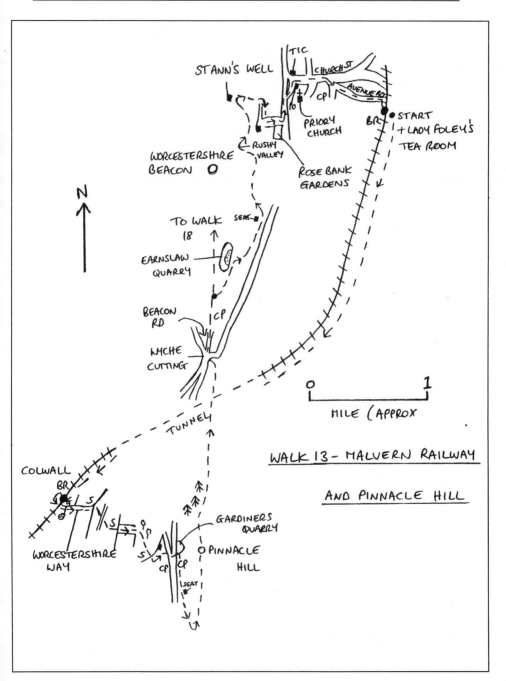

ST ANN'S WELL

TIC

CHURCH ST

AVENUE RD

CP

PRIORY CHURCH

BR

START
+ LADY FOLEY'S
TEA ROOM

WORCESTERSHIRE
BEACON O

RUSHY VALLEY

ROSE BANK
GARDENS

N

TO WALK
18

SEAT

EARNSLAW
QUARRY

BEACON
RD

CP

WYCHE
CUTTING

0   1

MILE (APPROX

TUNNEL

WALK 13 - MALVERN RAILWAY

COLWALL
BR

AND PINNACLE HILL

S

S

S

GARDINERS
QUARRY

WORCESTERSHIRE
WAY

S

CP

CP

O PINNACLE
HILL

SEAT

on a surfaced track to reach a circular stone marker, labelled Gold Mine. Since the 18th century, various attempts have been made to extract copper, tin and gold on this site, although nothing of great value was ever found.

Here, depending on how energetic you feel, you have the choice of continuing on the surfaced path to the summit of Worcestershire Beacon, joining Walk 18 at point [**], for a **longer walk** of 6½ miles. For the **shorter route**, turn right at the circular marker, taking the path at 2 o'clock, signed Quarry Walk. This drops through trees and levels out to reach a fork in the path. Continue ahead alongside a low stone wall and then down through trees to an open area. The steps on the left lead to a viewing platform over Earnslaw Quarry where a pool now occupies the quarry floor. With your back to the quarry and a fallen tree to the left, go ahead downhill on a wide path. This drops almost to road level by a seat before continuing ahead uphill on what is, I promise, the last climb of the day.

The terrace path climbs steadily through trees across the lower slopes of Worcestershire Beacon. Ignore any paths on either side and continue around the head of the scree covered Rushy valley to reach St Ann's Well (see Walk 18 for details). Turn right in front of the building and it's all downhill from now on! Go down the zig-zag tarmac path to a road. Turn right and go down steps, left of the drive ahead, to Rose Bank Gardens. Cross the road and bear left downhill past a sign to the station, and a post office. At the corner, (tourist office opposite), turn right down Church Street and right again down Avenue Road to the railway station.

Walk 14. Mamble and Bayton

Start/parking: County Council picnic place and parking area on A456 near the turning for Mamble, grid reference 685 713.

Distance: 4½ miles

Summary: Delightfully varied circuit over mixed farmland, through several wooded dingles, mature parkland and two lovely villages. Beautiful views are a particular feature of this generally well waymarked walk. Plenty of mud in winter and, currently, several awkward gates. 15 stiles (some quite rickety).

Maps: Landranger 138, Pathfinder 952.

Public transport: Limited bus service from Cleobury Mortimer, Bewdley and Kidderminster. Not daily and not on Sundays.

1-1-2000 - Sunny but cold day very muddy - (over boots) and Kizzy. good walk, very rural worcestershire landscape.

The Tea Shop

Craft Centre, Mamble.

Mamble Craft Centre occupies sensitively restored 17th century barns. The Centre houses several craft workshops offering demonstrations of traditional crafts such as picture framing, needlework, soft furnishings, curtains, and painting. For those interested in learning a new skill, courses are available. The complex stands on the edge of the village with glorious views to the Clee Hills. The tea room annexe is very welcoming and in fine weather you can sit outside overlooking the courtyard or on the lawn facing the superb view. Try the baked potatoes and toasted sandwiches with an extensive range of fillings, including the more unusual chicken tikka, stilton and bacon. Salads and soup, together with cream teas and gateaux are also available, all at reasonable prices. A delicious array of home-made cakes will make you dally at the counter where the choice includes caramel and vanilla slices, lemon meringue and doughnuts. Open all year with free admission and parking. Tuesday to Saturday, 10.30am to 5.00pm and 11.30am to 5.30pm on Sundays and Bank Holidays. Tel: 01299 832834.

Mamble Craft Centre

The Walk

From the picnic site, return to the main road, cross over and turn right. At the turning to Mamble village, look for the footpath sign just beyond the junction. Go left up steps and over a stile into a field. Head half right and cross a stile between a shed and a house. Go down the alleyway to the road and bear left to the village hall. Turn right and in 20 metres, turn left down the drive by Richmond House. Go through the gate at the end into a field. Follow the hedge on the left and cross a stile by a gate. Head half right across the field to cross another stile by electricity poles.

Go straight over this narrow field, crossing the stile ahead. Away to the left are Brown Clee and Titterstone Clee Hills, the latter with its giant golfball on the summit. This glorious view will stay with you for much of the walk and you may see buzzards soaring high overhead. In areas where pockets of woodland still survive, these majestic birds of prey can flourish and breed more easily than in a typical farmland prairie desert. Walking in Worcestershire over the years, I've been heartened to see that buzzards seem to be spreading further afield. Years ago, it was very unusual to spot them much further east than the Wyre Forest but now I even see them near my home, over the border in Warwickshire.

Continue downhill to the bottom right corner of the field. Cross the stile and footbridge over the stream. Climb up the next field, heading for two stiles in the top right corner. Cross the left stile, ignore the stile immediately right, and head downhill alongside the tree line on the right. At the bottom, stick close to the edge of the grassy bank by the stream and watch for a muddy track down to another stile. Cross this and the footbridge. Climb the bank and keep the fence on the right up through trees. At the top, you'll have to climb a metal gate. Continue ahead through the trees to a large field.

Turn left to the corner, then right along the field edge (hedge on the left). Cross the stile at the top corner and continue, hedge still on the left. Climb another awkward gate into the next field. Follow the fence on the left uphill to climb a stile at the top (mind the barbed wire) onto the road. Turn left through the village of Bayton, a treasure house of magpie architecture. At a T-junction, turn left, passing the Wheatsheaf Inn (now closed). When the road bears right, look for a marker post and turn right alongside the primary school. Follow the lane to St Bartholomew's church, boasting an impressive Norman font and a superb east window. Go through a gate at the rear of the churchyard, where glorious views open out again. Head half left downhill to go through a gate onto a tarmac lane.

Turn left and follow the lane for a mile, past Mayberries Farm and the Shakenhurst estate lodge and notice the distinctive elegance of the Hall ahead. Cross the cattle grid and continue on the lane for about half a mile. Just past the start of a new plantation (left), and a mature oak alongside the lane, turn left and cross the stile in the fence into a field. Head downhill to the bottom right corner, cross the stile and join the forest road directly ahead. Turn left and follow the track over the bridge across Shakenhurst Brook. Just by a marker post on the other side, turn left along the muddy forest track. This climbs gradually and bends right, away from the brook.

Keep bearing right and emerge into an open area (past yellow arrows on a tree). Continue ahead, bearing left by a marker post (with a warning sign underneath which is, to say the least, alarming!). Continue on the stony track and just past another sign by a pheasant enclosure, the track becomes grassy. Ignore the left bend and continue ahead through the edge of the wood, past a marker and round a gate into a field. Turn right and cross a stile in the next fence, then head for the top left corner of the field. Go through a gate and bear half left to go through a gate in the top left corner. Cross the driveway and go

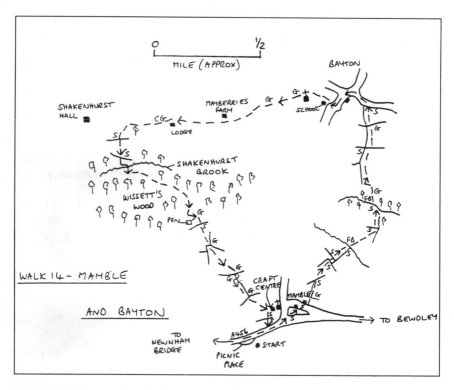

through the gate immediately on the right. Turn left and follow the hedge on the left, through a muddy gateway at the corner to see the Craft Centre. On a day of sticky heat interspersed with showers, plagued by horse flies and herds of frisky cattle, this was an oasis! A stile just right of the Centre leads to it and Mamble village.

Just beyond the Centre is St John's church, whose simple beauty is complemented by a remarkable tower, partly wooden and topped with a witch's hat spire, so common in the Teme valley. The now-blocked Crusader door enabled knights on horseback to receive a blessing before dashing off to the Crusades. It hardly seems worth the effort of manoeuvring a horse into a church for such a purpose, although it was probably intended more to impress the ladies. A Roman Catholic chapel, an unusual attachment to the rear of the church, is currently being restored by English Heritage. Return to the stile in front of the Centre, and turn left along the field to go through a gate. Cross the stile by houses ahead and rejoin the road near the picnic place.

Walk 15. Overbury, Bredon Hill and Kemerton

Start/parking: Side streets near the church in Overbury but please do not obstruct the lane by the church on Sundays. Start the walk from the church lychgate, grid reference 957 374.

Distance: 6½ miles

Summary: A marvellous walk with superb views over Bredon Hill and through the charming villages of Overbury, Conderton and Kemerton. Excellent footpaths throughout with 6 stiles.

Maps: Explorer 14, OS Landranger 150.

Public transport: As for Walk 1, daily buses (except Sunday or bank holidays) from Tewkesbury, Cheltenham and Evesham, which is also the nearest railway station from which buses run, calling at Overbury, Kemerton and Conderton, so you can join the walk at any of these villages.

The Tea Shop

The Coffee Shop, Elaine Rippon Silk Centre, Conderton.

Visitors to Broadway and Stratford upon Avon may have noticed the Elaine Rippon shops which stock a selection of hand painted silk, everything from scarves and ties to waistcoats. The whole range is designed and produced at the Studio in Conderton, where visitors are welcome to watch the work in progress. Opposite the studio is the Coffee Shop where you can enjoy tea, coffee and soft drinks together with a small, but delicious range of cakes, all reasonably priced. The tables overlook the courtyard and the walls are adorned with silk pictures, while colourful pottery and plants complete the cheerful scene. Open Monday to Saturday 10.30am-5.00pm all year, except over Xmas and New Year. Tel: 01386 725289.

The Walk

Overbury is a gem of a village with honey-coloured stone the equal

Cherry blossom, St Faith's churchyard

of anything in the Cotswolds. The cottages, their gardens a riot of colour, lie scattered along narrow lanes winding up Bredon Hill. Overbury Manor, with its elegant Georgian facade, has been lived in by the Holland-Martin family for centuries and much of the village and its cottages remain part of the Overbury Estate. Inside St Faith's church are many features of interest and unusually, the lychgate houses the impressive war memorial. The churchyard boasts a magnificent spring display of magnolia and cherry trees. The stream, which once provided enough power to run six mills, now trickles through the village before flowing into a tranquil pond.

From the lychgate, turn left and right in front of Overbury Manor and at a T-junction, turn left. After 100 metres, turn right by a signpost and go down a drive to cross a stone stile between yew trees. Follow the right edge of the field alongside first a wall, then the bowling green. At the end of the field, bear right into trees and follow the path to the road. Turn left into Conderton. On the left is Conderton Pottery, housed in the Old Forge, where Toff Milway produces and sells a wide range of stoneware pottery. A few metres further on is the Silk Centre. Just past the pub, turn left and almost

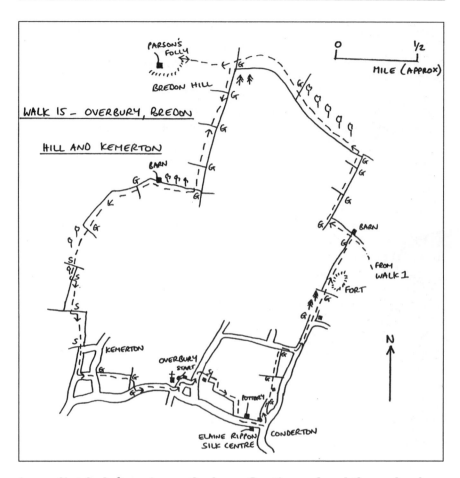

immediately left again up the lane. Continue ahead through a broken gate into an orchard, which may have been the site of the original settlement. Pass left of a barn, heading for the left of two gates in the far wall. Go through, then keep the wall on the right to go through another gate at the end onto a road.

Turn right and at the next corner, go left up a farm track. Where the lane curves right, continue ahead through a gate and alongside a plantation. The path climbs steadily, through another gate, with an old fort to the right, before reaching a ruined barn in the top corner. (Here we intersect with part of Walk 1). Turn left through a gate, keep ahead (wall on the right) to go through another gate. Turn right, (wall on the right) and go through another gate ahead. Continue ahead through two more gates, then turn left between trees and a fence. At the end of the trees, go through a gate and continue (fence on the left), to pass a plantation and go through another gate. (Aim for Parson's Folly ahead and enjoy the magnificent view from the summit, before returning to the gate but don't go through). Turn right with the wall on the left through three more gates to join a farm track, which leads ahead through another gateway. Turn right, with the hedge on the right and go past a barn. Ignore a stile on the right, continue on the farm track through a gate and keep the hedge on the right.

Ignore the first gate (right), but pass through the next. Continue ahead, downhill in a grassy hollow following a line of trees on the right. In the dip, climb up the grassy path, still following the trees to a stile by a gate. Go through the trees and emerge into a field and a junction of several tracks. Keep left and in 50 metres, go over a stile on the left. Turn right alongside the wall and cross a stile in the top corner. Turn left along the track and at the corner, turn right downhill with the hedge on the left. Cross a stile at the bottom onto a lane in Kemerton, a delightful village of Cotswold stone and thatched cottages. A stream, burbling past the cottages, provides a charming accompaniment as you walk ahead through the village. After half a mile, take the first left and at the T-junction, go through the gate opposite into a field. Keep the hedge on the left to go through a kissing gate at the end and bear half right to the road. Turn left to return to Overbury church.

Walk 16. Pershore and Tyddesley Wood

Start/parking: Long-stay parking behind the Abbey church. The walk starts from outside Carleton House Coffee Shop, grid reference 951 454. Alternative parking at Pershore bridge picnic place, just off A44 or by Tiddesley Wood, grid reference 929 459, so you can join the walk at either point.

Distance: 5 miles

Summary: Enjoyable, undemanding, circuit from a town rich in history, alongside the River Avon and through the sylvan delights of Tyddesley Wood. A riverside safari through summer growth can be quite entertaining but this is generally a well waymarked walk, albeit a trifle muddy underfoot. 9 stiles.

Maps: Explorer 14, Landranger 150.

Public transport: BR station just 2 miles north of town almost in Pinvin with trains from Hereford, Malvern, Worcester, Oxford and London Paddington. Frequent buses from Worcester, Broadway, Great Malvern and Evesham. No Sunday service.

The Tea Shop

The Carleton Coffee Shop, Bridge Street, Pershore.

Just a short walk from the bustling square and Abbey church, Carleton House offers a tempting range of home baked meals. There is a very welcome no smoking room and the pine tables occupy two levels. The atmosphere is restful with old clocks adorning the walls, and paintings by local artists on sale. The menu includes soup, jacket potatoes, toasted sandwiches and a daily specials board. Sample the mouth-watering array of home made cakes including lemon meringue, apricot crumble and scones or tea cakes. Open: 9.00am-5.00pm every day except Thursday and Sunday. Tel: 01386 554235.

Pershore Abbey

The Walk

Pershore is a storehouse of ancient and modern architecture from the historic precincts of the Abbey amid a scattering of centuries old buildings, to the thriving shopping centre. Many of the facades are Georgian and several arched entrances survive from the days of coaching traffic. Pershore is another town that owes much of its history and layout to the River Severn, which curls around it in a great loop. The old bridge is spared the weight of modern traffic by a more recent span, built alongside. During the Civil War, Royalist soldiers attempted to blow up the original bridge in an attempt to halt the advance of Cromwell's troops.

Grand though the Abbey seems today, it is but a shadow of its former self, a once mighty edifice similar in size to Tewkesbury. Most of the Abbey was destroyed during the Dissolution. Look at the exterior of the building and you can still see traces of the earlier monastic buildings. A line of trees marks the position of the nave and the outline of an arch is quite visible on one wall. The blocked doorway on the south wall allowed monks access to the church from their cells. The interior seems flooded with light and you can appreciate the skill of the masons who created the magnificent chancel and vaulted roof adorned with carved bosses. The Lantern Tower contains an unusual bell ringing platform, suspended high above the congregation.

Turn right from Carleton House down Bridge Street to the river. Turn right to follow a footpath (signed to Tiddesley Wood) alongside the river. Walk through a gate, under power lines and within a mile, cross two footbridges. Ignore the first path right and keep alongside the river on a path, which can be overgrown. Cross a third footbridge and turn half right over the field to cross a stile by a gate onto the A4104. Turn right along the verge. After 100 metres, cross this busy road and follow the bridleway up the lane. At the end, go through a gate to the right of a thatched cottage. Ignore the footpath (right) and continue ahead on the bridleway leading to a stile by a metal gate. Go through the gate immediately beyond and follow the fence on the left to a gate into Tiddesley Wood.

Once part of the ancient wildwood, Tiddesley was used by locals as a source of timber, as a deer park and as a foraging area for their pigs. The wood is now cared for by the Worcestershire Wildlife Trust who have re-introduced traditional methods of forestry. Part

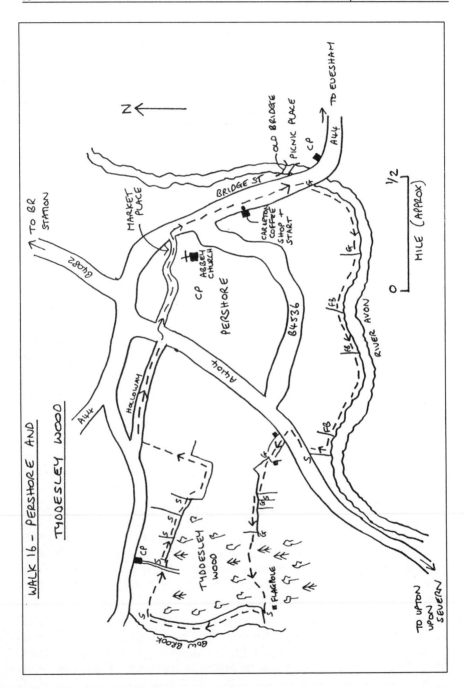

WALK 16 – PERSHORE AND TYDDESLEY WOOD

of the southern section is occupied by a rifle range, so keep well away from this end of the wood when red flags are flying. Butterflies dance along the sunlit, open paths and the superb habitat supports healthy populations of birds such as blackcaps and garden warblers. These delicate birds sound remarkably similar and it takes a keen ear to detect the differences in their bubbling songs. Fortunately, they look completely different, the blackcap living up to its name with a neat, black skullcap, while the garden warbler is distinctive only for its lack of markings. Tiddesley's greatest treasure is its range of flowering plants with over 300 species recorded.

Keep ahead on the sometimes muddy bridleway, ignoring any cross tracks. Just past a rifle range flagpole, turn right over a stile into a field with Bow Brook at the bottom. Walk ahead alongside the wood at the top of a field, ablaze with buttercups and daisies in the summer. Pass two orchards and enjoy views to the Malverns. At the end of the wood, turn right back into the wood. (You can cross the stile and turn right up steps if you wish, but there's a gap which makes this unnecessary). Follow the path just inside the left edge of the wood to reach a wide cross track with the car park to the left.

Turn left and immediately right, over a stile and follow the path along the right edge of the field, parallel with the wood, over three stiles. After the third stile, walk up a bank and bear right on a clear headland. This path swings left alongside a fence and at the next signpost, by a metal gate, turn left on a wide track between fields. Views open out once again to the Malverns and the Abbey. To show how gradually you've climbed, you are disconcertingly level with the top of its tower. The track emerges onto a road (Holloway). Turn right down the hill and at the end (note the wagon wheel on the side of a house), turn left and take the first right. Follow this road to Abbey Park where a left turn leads back to the Market Place and Bridge Street.

Walk 17. Spetchley Park

Start/parking: Use a small layby on A422 by Spetchley Park, grid reference
                     898 538, while you complete the walk. Please use the small
                     car park at the gardens only while visiting them.

Distance: 4 miles

Summary: Undemanding exploration of mixed farmland to the south of
                     Spetchley Gardens, partly across parkland, through woodland
                     and across a wildflower meadow. Waymarking is poor, there is
                     a locked gate to climb and 3 stiles.

Maps: Landranger 150, Pathfinder 996.

Public transport: Limited bus service from Worcester, Redditch and Alcester
                     (Saturdays only). Nearest BR station at Worcester.

The Tea Shop

Tea Room, Spetchley Park Gardens.

Inside the grounds, the Tea Room occupies an old laundry overlooking a pleasant lawn, surrounded by trees. Managed by Clive and Beryl Bagley since 1991, it's renowned for the excellence of its home-made cakes, hardly surprising really when you consider they also run a business selling Beryl's cakes. A tempting selection is available along with ice cream, hot chocolate, coffee and generous pots of tea (a tea cosy is a welcome touch). Groups can be catered for if you telephone two or three days in advance, when a more comprehensive menu, including sandwiches, cream teas and salads, can be arranged.

The Tea Room, obviously tied to the garden hours, currently opens 12.00noon-5.00pm, and 11.00am at Easter and 2.00pm on Sundays. The gardens open from April to the end of September between 11.00am-5.00pm Tuesday to Friday plus Bank Holiday Mondays and Sundays between 2.00am-5.00pm. Bad weather may deter garden visitors and in such circumstances, it's not worth keeping the tea room open. Tel: 01905 345213/224 for gardens and 01386 792774 or 0585 187491 for Beryl and Clive Bagley.

The Walk

Spetchley Park Gardens boasts many rare plants, trees and shrubs. Both the Hall, which is not open to visitors, and the gardens belong to the Berkeley family, who also own Berkeley Castle in Gloucestershire. Several visits will allow you to appreciate the dazzling display of flowers; there's always something different to see throughout spring and summer. The gardens are very intimate, a series of hidden corners and sheltered nooks revealing a changing scene at every turn. Several unusual features include the strangest Adam and Eve you are ever likely to see. For a start, they're fully clothed in 17th century French costume with not a fig leaf in sight! The nearby Root House is made entirely of wood, with gnarled trunks and a thatched roof.

Unusually clad statue of Adam, Spetchley Park Gardens

From the layby, head west towards Worcester along the A422. Walk this first half mile on pavement quickly to escape the speeding traffic. Pass All Saints church and on reaching a "Tractors turning sign", cross over to go up steps and cross two stiles into a field. Head half right, parallel with the fence on the right to the top right corner of the field. Cross the stile in the fence and head half right. Aim for the left end of pine trees on the right, to a metal gate (**not** the stile into the wood, nor the secong gate further left). At the time of writing, this gate was arrowless and padlocked, but the public

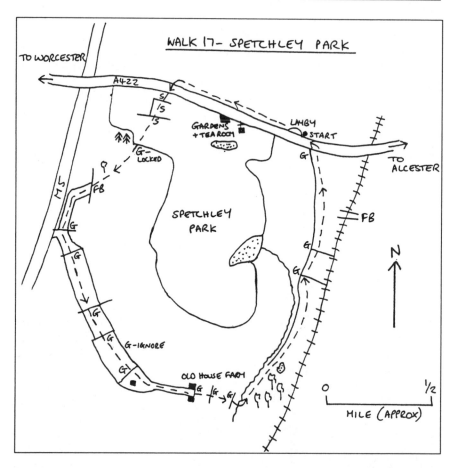

WALK 17- SPETCHLEY PARK

TO WORCESTER

A422

TO ALCESTER

LAMBY START

GARDENS + TEA ROOM

G-LOCKED

FB

M5

G

G

SPETCHLEY PARK

G

G-IGNORE

OLD HOUSE FARM

G

FB

G

G

G

N

0   ½
MILE (APPROX)

footpath does go through here (if it's still locked, you'll have to climb this awkward obstacle).

In the next field, if crops permit, head half left passing left of a lone tree in the general direction of the M5, with the Malverns as a far more enticing backdrop. At the bottom of the field, cross a concrete bridge over a stream and follow the green lane towards the M5. Don't panic, I'm not sending you across it! This path joins a concrete lane just before the motorway, which bends left alongside it. (Earplugs at the ready here!). Go through the gate and turn left (not the under-pass) onto a wide stony track, an unsigned bridleway. Walk ahead and go straight through the first metal gate across the lane. Keep in the same direction, roughly south east (ignore gate to left), to go through a handgate by an iron gate and in 50 metres, pass your first blue arrow (hallelujah!). The lane narrows to a path between trees and at the next junction, go through a muddy gateway ahead to the right of an iron gate.

Continue on the narrow path through nettles to a field. Turn left along the tree line, ignore the metal gate (left) and head for the top left corner of the field, with a house (right). Go through the handgate (more lovely mud) and follow this rutted path to a drive by a marker post. Turn left along the farm track towards Old House Farm. Walk straight through the farmyard, passing left of a metal barn. Go through a gate into a field, through another wobbly gate ahead and on through a third directly ahead by a wood. Turn immediately left through a delightful green tunnel of trees between the wood and a stream. This is the loveliest part of the walk, if a trifle muddy, and you emerge by a pond into a meadow which, in summer, is full of wildflowers.

Several faint horse tracks continue ahead (generally north), parallel to the hedge and stream (left) and the railway (right). Keep to the highest part of the field and when you can see the railway tracks emerging from the cutting on the right, head slightly left to a gate in the top left corner. Continue ahead along the left edge of the field on a path which is an entertaining mixture of mud, ruts, prickles and nettles, depending on the season! Keep ahead through the next gateway and follow the hedge (left) through the next field. Along the way you see a railway footbridge off to the right, although there's no sign of the footpath which should lead to it. The track you are on reaches a gate onto the A422, where, with some relief, you can turn left to the layby. If you've done the walk, as we did, on a hot day, you'll be more than ready for some of Beryl's cakes and a cup of tea!

Walk 18. St Ann's Well and Worcestershire Beacon

Start: As for Walks 7 and 13, from the railway station, Great Malvern, grid reference 783 457.

Distance: 6 miles

Summary: An exhilarating walk with outstanding views. Although there is considerable up and down, we use one of the easiest paths up Worcestershire Beacon. Paths are excellent and there are no stiles but you should be prepared for the difference in temperature at the top. In summer, it can be a welcome break from the heat but in winter, quite teeth chattering.

Maps: Explorer 14, Landranger No. 150. Local shops also stock a large scale version (1:10,000) covering the whole ridge in three maps.

Public transport: Same as for Walk 7.

The Tea Shop

St Ann's Well, Victoria Walk, Great Malvern.

St Ann's Well is perched halfway up the path to the Worcestershire Beacon and is very popular with walkers. The Well building looks much as it did when it was first built, between 1815 and 1819. It was originally used as a pump room for sampling the spring waters, with enough room to "put the affected part under the spout" – the mind boggles! In 1844, the Octagon Bar was opened to provide refreshments but by the 1960s, the almost derelict building was taken over by the Malvern Hills Conservators. There are many other springs scattered about the hills; St John's and Holy Well are two of the better known ones.

Rosalind Redman has lived here for seven years and offers a vegetarian menu, with hot meals available from 11.00am-3.30pm. The atmosphere is welcoming and cheerful and you can sit outside on the terrace overlooking the spring in a delightful setting with splendid views towards the town. The tasty menu includes home made soup, baked potatoes, veggie burgers, pies, samosas, spring rolls and vegetarian bakes and salads. At other times a delicious range of home-made cakes is available. Open: daily from 10.00am-6.00pm from Easter to end September, from 10.00am to dusk at weekends from October until Easter. Tel: 01684 560285

Circular signpost near Sugarloaf Hill

The Walk

The motto chosen by Great Malvern Town Council from Psalm 121 is particularly appropriate, "I will lift up mine eyes unto the hills", for wherever you are in the town, the Malverns are a constant back-drop. Depending on the weather, the hills display a remarkable range of colours, from a smoky blue silhouette to a vivid patchwork of greens, browns and purples with all manner of hues in between.

The Malvern Hills Conservators face an onerous task in caring for these hills. They are responsible for path maintenance, scrub clearance and the provision of seats and car parks, of which there are a good number. The Conservators were largely responsible for halting quarrying in the hills, before their profile was changed forever. George Bernard Shaw, ever at his pithiest, remarked that the hills would very soon become the Malvern Flats! The hills are very vulnerable to fire. During the recent scorching summers, huge areas have been ravaged by fires, some started deliberately and enormous damage can be done in a very short time.

Turn right from the station and, at the junction, left up Avenue Road to Church Street. Turn left uphill and emerge below Belle Vue Terrace. Cross over to Lloyds Bank, turn left and right into Rose Bank Gardens. Go up the steps to St Ann's Road. Go ahead up the drive, cross the road and go left by a footpath sign. This tarmac path zig-zags uphill to St Ann's Well. Turn right behind the building and at a path junction by a seat, turn left. In 20 metres, turn left again by another seat onto a wide, grassy path which climbs steadily, enjoying expansive views over Great Malvern. We'll follow this path in long zig-zags to the summit of Worcestershire Beacon but please don't take any of the shortcuts. As you can see, erosion is a serious problem and, in any case, the steeper paths are hell on the knees and lungs.

Pass four seats (vandals permitting!), and by the fifth, turn sharp right, still on the wide path but at an easier gradient (now heading in the direction of North Hill). At the next corner, zig-zag left and round the next corner where the toposcope on the Beacon appears ahead. You can also see our remaining zig-zags crossing the face of it! At the fourth seat, you can see Pinnacle Hill, climbed on Walk 13. Turn right, continue climbing and the path emerges onto a stonier path. Turn left on the last zig (or zag?) to the surfaced path by the summit of Worcestershire Beacon, with its triangulation point, toposcope and terrace where a café once stood. This is where the longer option from **Walk 13 joins (**)**.

At 425 metres, you can stand no higher in the entire county. The views are exhilarating, almost aerial, revealing a panorama of hills, woods, orchards, farmland and commons sprinkled with picturesque villages. Westward lie the rolling hills of Herefordshire with the Welsh Black Mountains looming in the distance, while to the north rise the isolated outcrops of Abberley and Kinver Edge. Bredon Hill stands sentinel over the Vale of Evesham while the Cotswolds and Severn estuary beckon further south. The flatness of the Worcester plain contrasts sharply with the gently rolling, wooded countryside to the west.

Geologically, these hills present a puzzle. The ridge is obviously composed of harder rock than the surrounding plain or we would not be standing so high above it. These rocks are among the oldest on earth, (formed long before the simplest life forms crawled out of the primordial slime) and, as such, contain no fossils. If it's possible to grasp such figures, they are more than 600 million years old (give or take a week or two!). Various fault lines crossing the hills correspond to passes which now carry roads and footpaths.

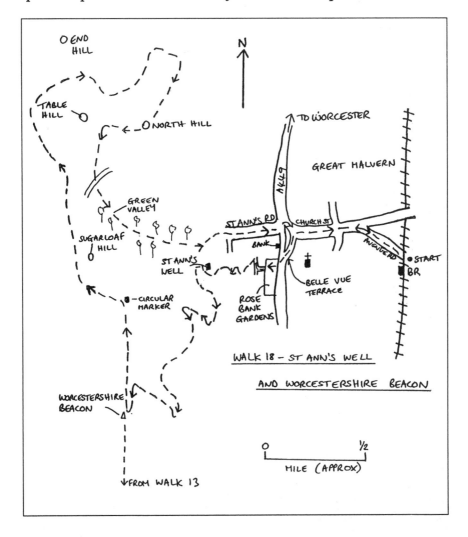

From the summit, head north and drop gradually downhill towards the hills ahead – Sugarloaf on the left and North Hill on the right. We skirt the former and climb the latter. Take any of the parallel paths downhill to a path junction by a circular stone marker on the col before Sugarloaf. Take the path at 11 o'clock, signed Sugarloaf, which passes left of the hill, past three seats. When the path starts to curve back, head left past a bench and take the second path left (not the first left steeply downhill). Walk past a seat and go gradually downhill with views over West Malvern.

Turn right on reaching the lower path and start to climb again, curving round the far end of the hill to pass the head of a valley. The hill to the left is End Hill at the northernmost end of the ridge. Ignore the first right fork in the path and after half a mile, at a second fork, take the right hand, higher path which rounds North Hill. When you come to a barbed wire fence and Malvern appears below, take a grassy path on the right. This climbs steeply, turning right at a mini rock outcrop on a wide path to the summit of North Hill, another outstanding viewpoint. See if you can pick out Clee Hill, the Wrekin and Wenlock Edge in Shropshire and the Clent and Lickey Hills near Birmingham. From the summit, turn right downhill to the col between North Hill and Table Hill. At the col, turn left downhill through gorse and birch trees (ignore paths branching right) to a wide path.

Cross straight over, down steps and follow a grassy path down Green Valley. During spring and autumn, the trees and scrub in this valley provide valuable shelter for migrating birds such as ring ouzels, the mountain equivalent of our blackbird. They are slightly bigger than the blackbird but with a white breast band. Also during autumn, you may see snow buntings passing through. They spend the breeding season high on Scottish mountains and this mini-range must seem rather tame compared to the wild grandeur of the Cairngorms. The track reaches a tarmac path. Continue downhill past houses and emerge onto St Ann's Road. Continue downhill back into Great Malvern.

Walk 19. Tenbury Wells

Start/parking: Free car parking just off Teme Street, grid reference 595 684.

Distance: 4½ miles

Summary: Varied undulating circuit offering glorious views across the Teme valley, through woodland and orchards with a return across farmland. Watch the skies because buzzards are plentiful. Waymarking is adequate, some paths are unclear and there are 18 stiles.

Maps: Landranger 138, Pathfinder 972.

Public transport: Regular buses from Worcester, Bromyard, Cleobury Mortimer, Hereford, Kidderminster, Leominster, Stourport and Ludlow but no Sunday service.

The Tea Shop

Tabs Tea Room, Teme Street, Tenbury Wells

A popular venue overlooking the main street, Tabs offers a warm welcome. The wide range of goodies on offer includes a full English breakfast served each morning, plus jacket potatoes and sandwiches which you can also take away. Lunches include a delicious broccoli and stilton crumble while smaller portions for children round off a menu which caters for all tastes. For those blessed, (or cursed depending upon your current weight), with a sweet tooth a tempting range of desserts and cakes is available. Open 9.00am-5.00pm Monday to Saturday all year, also 12.00noon-5.00pm Sunday in summer. Tel: 01584 811712.

The Walk

The bustling market town of Tenbury Wells has always been known as the "Town in the Orchard." Although many orchards have disappeared, Tenbury is still surrounded by a dazzling display of blossom each spring. Return to the main car park entrance, and turn right along Teme Street past the post office. Cross and go down the alley-

St Mary's, Tenbury

way left of the Regal Centre to the church. In the 18th century, St
Mary's may have regretted its proximity to the river Teme, which
flows past the churchyard. The river burst its banks, flooding all in
its path and reaching a considerable depth inside the church, de-
stroying much of the building in the process. A plaque inside the
chancel recalls the devastation which left only the tower, north wall
and chancel. The church was rebuilt in the 1770s. A remarkable
stone effigy, called the Little Crusader, can be seen inside and, just to
even things out, there is a Big Crusader.

Walk past either side of the church, to the far corner of the churchyard (not the main gates left). Go through a green gate into the
churchyard extension, and turn left through another gate. Turn right
along the alleyway to bungalows, and continue ahead to an estate
road, which bears left. Just past an electricity pole, turn right over a
footbridge and stile into a meadow. Just before you reach the next
hedge line, bear left to the top left corner and through a small gate in
the corner. This alleyway leads to Berrington Road through a gate
which is a bit of a squeeze (I think all those teashops were catching
up with me!).

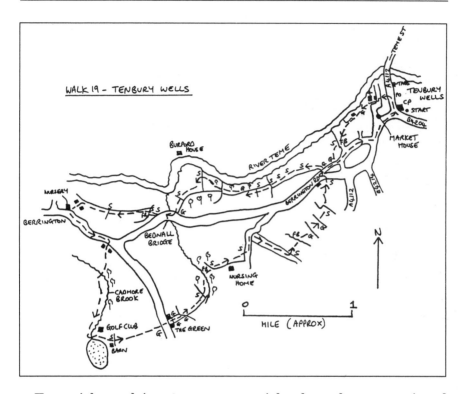

Turn right and in 50 metres, go right through a gate, signed
Bednall Bridge. This narrow way, behind houses, bears left to cross a
stile. Keep the hedge on the right and in the top right corner, continue along a narrow, overgrown path behind gardens. After two
more stiles, and after doing a troglodyte impression, emerge into another meadow. Cross the third stile ahead and follow the hedge on
the right to cross another stile. Walk ahead to appreciate the splendid view across the valley which stretches as far as Clee Hill with its
"golf ball" awaiting a mighty tee shot, round to the wooded hills
above Ludlow further west. The River Teme is nearby but completely hidden in the trees at the foot of this steep escarpment. Continue along the edge to go through a gate into the wood. Follow this
muddy path along the edge and when the path emerges into the
open, by a marker post, turn right downhill.

At the bottom, bear left over a stile and walk between the wood
(left) and the nursery trees (right). The splendid residence on the opposite side of the river is Burford House, whose gardens are open to

the public. Ignore any stiles (left) and in the top left corner, cross a stile by a gate and follow the track. This bends left to a lane by Bednall Bridge. Turn right over the bridge and in 50 metres, go right over a stile. Turn left along the hedge and where this bends left, keep ahead to a gap in the tree line. Cross the plank bridge and stile into another orchard. Follow the fence on the right to cross a stile by a metal gate into the nursery. Continue ahead on the surfaced track, bending right with the fence. Where the track forks, by a signpost, bear left through greenhouses and past a house to the lane. Turn left along the lane, ignore the first stile (right) and, in half a mile, turn right between houses. Go downhill on a rough track to cross a bridge and immediately turn left. This track leads alongside fields and a stream to a surfaced lane at the golf course.

Continue ahead to the lake and bear left. Pass right of the hotel, (lake on your right) and at the corner of the lake, bear left uphill past a timber barn. Cross the stile and walk straight uphill between houses and through a gate to a lane. Continue ahead through The Green farm, using two black metal gates to enter a field beyond. Continue with the hedge on the left and in 50 metres, go through a gateway to the left, bearing a quiverful of arrows. Continue (hedge on the right) downhill to the bottom right corner. Ignore a stile (right) and cross the stile ahead into the wood. Continue downhill, bending left to cross a footbridge. What goes down must go up! Now regain all that height via a path up through the wood and cross a stile into a field. The path should go half right, heading for the top left corner of the field but was cropped on my visit. If necessary, follow the hedge on the right, past Haresbrook Nursing Home. Work your way round the field edge to cross the stile in the top left corner onto a drive.

Turn left and take the first right, by a bridleway sign. After half a mile, go over a stile on the left and head half left to cross a footbridge under a line of willow trees ahead. Bear right and go through the gate. Follow the electricity lines across the next two fields, through an awkward gate and cross the stile directly ahead. In the third field, bear half left, to cross a stile in the hedge, just past the houses. Turn left to Berrington Road and right down hill to pass the gates we used earlier. Here you can either follow your outward route back, or continue down the road into Tenbury. If you follow the latter, you will pass the oval-shaped Market House, built in 1811, and used as a corn and butter market.

Walk 20. Upper Arley and Trimpley Reservoir

Start/parking: Large riverside car park at grid reference 764 803, but it's much easier to arrive on the Severn Valley Railway just across the river from which the directions start. See the Introduction for more information about the railway and contact numbers for timetable details. Alternative parking in Eymore Wood, partway round the walk, at grid reference 774 792.

Distance: 4 miles.

Summary: A lovely, undemanding walk alongside the river Severn to reservoirs before climbing through Eymore wood. There is a wealth of wildlife to look for, especially in spring. Well waymarked but can be muddy; with 3 stiles.

Maps: Landranger 138, Pathfinders 932 and 952.

Public transport: BR service to Kidderminster, then Severn Valley Railway to Upper Arley. Limited service in winter. Buses from Kidderminster and Bridgnorth but no Sunday service.

The Tea Shop

The Old Bakehouse, Upper Arley.

This is possibly the only tea shop in Worcestershire which offers a genuine Cornish cream tea, and delicious it is too! Until five years ago, Louvain Beer and her husband ran a hotel in the West Country and have brought this treat with them. They also run the neighbouring Post Office which, amongst other things, serves tempting ice cream. Both buildings overlook delightful river scenery and in warmer weather, you can sit outside on the terrace and watch the world go by. As well as cream teas, you can enjoy sandwiches, cakes, teacakes, ice creams, sausage rolls and, another Cornish import, pasties. Several speciality teas and coffee are on offer. Inside, it is refreshingly non smoking and the ambience is cosy and welcoming. Opening times vary and are dependent on the weather, and trains. It's best to check first but, as a general rule, The Old Bakehouse

opens most weekend afternoons. During school holidays and when
the Severn Valley Railway is operating, it opens most afternoons except Tuesdays. Tel: 01299 861201

The Walk

If you arrive by train, the first thing you'll notice is the beautifully
maintained station at Arley, which has been used as the location for
the BBC TV series "Oh, Dr Beeching". The Severn Valley Railway
runs through some of the loveliest scenery in the county and villages
along the line, such as Upper Arley, Highley and Hampton Loade,
together with the towns of Bewdley and Bridgnorth receive large
numbers of visitors each year, all arriving by train. As well as providing a superb day out, this manages to keep a fair number of cars off
the road which can only be a good thing.

From the station, turn left down the road to Upper Arley village.
The glory of this picturesque backwater is in its idyllic, sylvan setting alongside the Severn. Ducks and swans beg for food by the old
bridge and in summer, swallows and martins swoop for insects over
the water. Overlooking the village from a hill at the edge of Arley estate is the 12th century church of St Peter's. Cross the only blot on
the landscape, the ugly footbridge, built in 1971 to replace a ferry.
Turn right alongside the river where you are now on both the Severn
Way and the Worcestershire Way. Follow the riverside path behind
houses, over a stile to cross a footbridge. Ignore the Worcestershire
Way going left and continue by the river where you can choose from
several parallel paths, depending on the level of mud. From here,
you can catch glimpses of the railway line but the biggest clue to its
presence is the piercing shriek from the whistle, accompanied by a
puff of smoke, rather like a giant, mobile kettle.

Cross a stile under Victoria Bridge, which carries the railway
across the river. After another stretch of woodland, cross another
stile bearing a strange warning, obviously designed for people with a
plaster of Paris fetish! Emerge into an open field by an information
board and the embankment to Trimpley Reservoir. Keep on the riverside path, and turn left by a marker post up onto the embankment.
Turn right alongside the reservoir. The cluster of modern buildings
is an eyesore, but I suppose that's the price of progress, or at least the
price of keeping Birmingham watered. One bonus for wildlife is the
reservoir's value to birds. During spring and autumn, many waders,

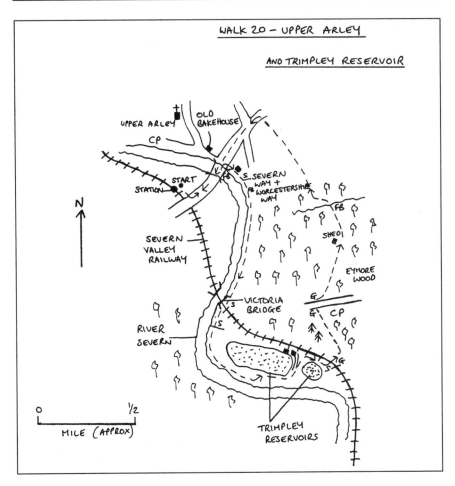

WALK 20 - UPPER ARLEY

AND TRIMPLEY RESERVOIR

terns and gulls may pause here on migration, so a quick scan with the binoculars could be worthwhile. At the far end, drop to the road between the reservoirs and turn left.

At the corner, turn right and continue with the lagoon on the right. This stretch, fringed by reeds, is free of boats and often has great crested grebes and tufted duck diving for food. The railway line is on the left, and just before the corner of the lagoon, turn left over a stile and cross the railway with care. Go through the gate into Eymore Wood and climb uphill. After 50 metres, bear left on the wider track. Eymore wood shelters a tremendous variety of birdlife, and most of the species found in the Wyre Forest can also be seen here. You pass conifers towering over a "dead" forest floor which contrasts markedly with the rich understorey beneath the mixed woodland opposite. This illustrates perfectly how vital it is for light to reach the forest floor to generate the growth of plants and flowers.

Ignore any paths to the right, and cross a grassy ride with views to the railway, reservoir and Wyre Forest beyond. Keep climbing and go through a gate onto a lane, by a car park (**). Go through the gate opposite back into the wood, on a bridleway. At the first junction, ignore the Worcestershire Way left, and continue ahead past a coloured marker post. At the next junction, keep ahead (blue/red marker), passing right of a metal shed. The path loses height and at the bottom, ignore the blue/red marker and cross the footbridge to meet the worst of the mud. Bear left (bridleway sign) and squelch alongside the stream before gaining height by the woodland edge. The track bears right away from the wood and goes between fields. Ignore any cross paths and continue ahead (hedge on the right) to a lane. Turn left downhill to the village.

Severn Valley Railway, Upper Arley

Walk 21. Upton upon Severn and the Hams

Start/parking: Car park off B4211, north of Upton Bridge, grid reference 850 407.

Distance: 4 miles

Summary: A pleasant easy walk south from Upton across farmland, returning alongside the River Severn through water meadows, where the Malverns form a magnificent backcloth. Lots of mud but waymarking is fairly good and there are 6 stiles, some awkward.

Maps: Landranger 150, Explorer 14.

Public transport: Regular buses from Worcester, Gloucester, Cheltenham, Great Malvern and Tewkesbury to Upton upon Severn. Nearest BR stations at Ashchurch, (near Tewkesbury) or Worcester, Great Malvern and Pershore.

The Tea Shop

Katie's Coffee Shop, Court Street, Upton upon Severn.

Owned by Jane Holder, Katie's offers a varied menu including an all day breakfast where you can have anything from a huge plateful to egg on toast, accompanied by toast, jam or marmalade and lashings of tea and coffee. Substantial hot snacks such as omelettes, toasted sandwiches and jacket potatoes satisfy lunchtime pangs, while salads, ploughman's and sandwiches are also available, along with a specials board. Baguettes and sandwiches are prepared to take away, a service which is very popular with local businesses. It's advisable to leave some space for the delicious desserts, such as bread pudding, apple pie and a variety of ice creams. A tempting range of home-made cakes, teacakes, muffins and scones should fill any remaining corners. Katie's has recently won an award from the "Good Café Guide". The atmosphere is cosy and welcoming, with a low beamed ceiling and it is non smoking. Open: weekdays 9.00am-4.00pm (closing at 2.00pm on Mondays) and

10.00am-5.00pm at weekends from December to March. From April to November, 8.00am-5.00pm on Saturday, 9.30am-5.00pm on Sunday and 9.00am-5.00pm weekdays (4.00pm on Thursday). Tel: 01684 592097.

The Walk

Upton upon Severn's history is inextricably linked to the River Severn. In the days when a trip by road was a long, nightmarish journey (not much different from today really!), the river provided a relatively fast means of carrying goods. It was not until the days of the railway that river transport became uneconomical and the trade died out. Ironically, the railway through Upton no longer exists, but river traffic, in the form of leisure craft, is increasing. During the summer, the river frontage with its popular pubs, bustling crowds and flowers, is a particularly colourful scene. Passenger boats, including the *MV Conway Castle*, run regular day and evening cruises.

Until the 14th century, a ferry was the only means of crossing this tempestuous waterway. Later, the flimsy wooden bridge was replaced by a stone structure, the first of many such replacements through the years. Even today the moods of the river and weather have a profound effect on the inhabitants of the town. Periods of heavy rain either locally or further upstream in the Welsh hills mean that the river can rise alarmingly, spilling over into the town and surrounding meadows.

Upton did not escape the consequences of the bloody English Civil War and on 29th August 1651, the Battle of Upton Bridge was fought. After a skirmish, the Parliamentarians regained possession of the bridge, securing this vital river crossing for Cromwell. The town's architecture is a superb blend of styles with remnants of timber framed, brick with Venetian windows and Georgian elegance. The variety of businesses is as diverse as the architecture and ranges from a specialist map shop to hand-made chocolates. One of the town's oldest buildings is the Tudor House Museum depicting Upton both past and present. Each year, Upton plays host to the lively, if rather bizarrely named, Oliver Cromwell Jazz Festival. The distinctive Bell Tower, or Pepperpot as it's affectionately known, is all that survives of the old riverside parish church. It was seriously damaged in the Civil War and, although various alterations were

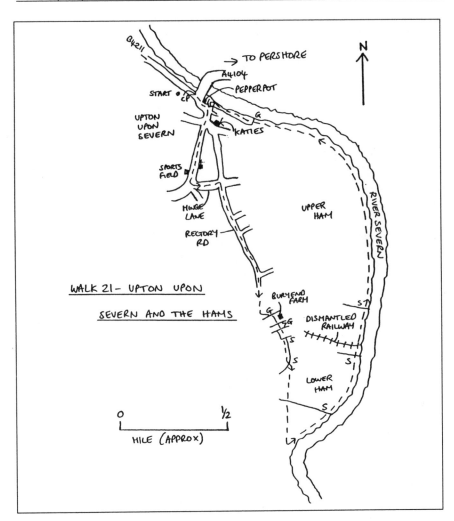

carried out, the spire was eventually declared unsafe and replaced by the unique cupola.

From the car park, turn right past the bridge and Pepperpot and right up the High Street out of town. Walk past St Peter and St Paul's church, which contains memorials from the old church. Opposite the sports field, by the fire station, turn left along Minge Lane. At the first crossroads, turn right along Rectory Road past Door Panels plc. At the end, where the road curves left, turn right down Buryend to Buryend Farm. Go through the gate and walk between the buildings,

MV Conway, Upton upon Severn

following the arrows. Go through another gate and a third just ahead, to walk with the hedge on the right to cross a stile by a gate into a field. Keep the hedge on the left to cross another stile at the end.

Walk ahead, crossing a wide ditch to the far fence. We were lucky enough to see a pair of little owls who scowled down at us from the nearby trees. Climb the awkward fence (I hesitate to call it a stile, and don't leave anything vital on the barbed wire!) into Lower Ham. The official footpath goes straight ahead to the riverside, but an un-official local shortcut has developed along the fence to the left. Whichever one you use, the aim is the same, to head for the riverside path. Turn left alongside the river through the Hams and over several stiles, passing the embankment of a dismantled railway. "Ham" derives from the Old English for meadow and this large area is often flooded in winter. As you move north, the full range of the Malverns rises up behind the town. The path eventually goes through a gate onto a lane which leads past the riverside pubs to the bridge and car park.

Walk 22. Upton upon Severn and Earls Croome

Start/parking: As for Walk 21, the car park near Upton Bridge, grid reference 850 407.

Distance: 5½ miles

Summary: An enjoyable circuit across farmland to Earls Croome village, followed by a trot down a bridleway through a wooded dingle. The River Severn is your companion through flood meadows back to Upton. Plenty of mud, waymarking could be improved and there are 10 stiles, some awkward.

Maps: Landranger 150, Explorer 14.

Public transport: Same as for Walk 21, with buses stopping at Ryall and Earls Croome on the route of the walk.

The Tea Shop

Old Bell House, New Street, Upton upon Severn.

This traditional tea room, run by Vi Hogan, occupies a striking building in the heart of Upton. The all day menu, on a blackboard on the wall, offers everything from cottage pie, roast beef, lamb or chicken to a traditional English breakfast and corned beef hash. Vegetarian chilli, lasagne, macaroni and cauliflower cheese is on offer, together with quiche and salad. Everything is home-made and the menu is changed from time to time with daily specials also available. Open every day from 10.00am-5.30pm. Tel: 01684 593828.

The Walk

Turn right from the car park and cross the bridge over the River Severn. At the end, cross over and go past Severn Way signs (which you ignore!). Walk ahead, left of the white house to reach a lane. Walk down the lane almost directly ahead, left of Bridge End House, to pass a footpath sign for Ryall (it would be more helpful if this were positioned back at the junction where it's needed!). The lane nar-

The Pepperpot

rows to cross the marina footbridge. Walk along an avenue of trees
and through a gate into the riverside meadows. Follow the path by
the river and through a squeeze stile at the end, where the path
winds left by a fence and through bungalows.

Go through a gate and turn left through the estate to a T-junction.
(At the time of writing, the footpath directly ahead was blocked by
the construction of new houses. Hopefully this may change and the
map details the footpath if you prefer it to the road). For now, turn
right along the road through Ryall and cross the A38 with great care
by the Bluebell Inn. Continue down the lane, bear left before the
Horse and Groom Inn and turn right down Green Lane. (If the earlier
footpath is accessible, this is where you'll rejoin the route).

At the end, turn left by the marker post and use the footbridge and
gate into a field. Turn right along the hedge, cross the footbridge and
continue ahead alongside the edge of a wood. After 100 metres, at
the brow of a hill, turn left along the highest part of the field, aiming
for a line of trees directly ahead. Cross the stile and continue ahead
with views to the Malverns. Cross a stile in the corner and aim for the
trees straight ahead and slightly downhill on a path where
head-high summer crops can be a struggle. Follow the wide track

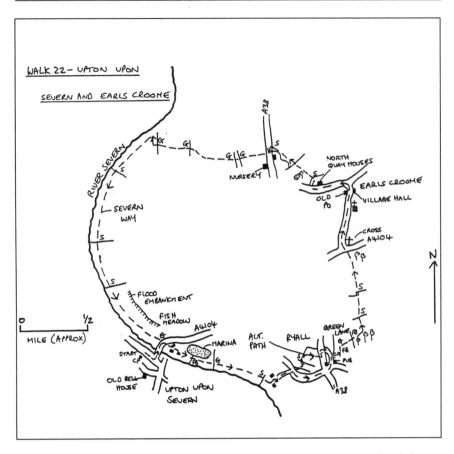

past trees to cross the A4104 and pass a memorial cross which has a particularly appropriate inscription.

Continue up the lane to Earls Croome, passing St Mary's church. Go past the village hall, and turn left at the junction by the old Post Office. After half a mile, turn right down an alleyway by North Quay houses. Go over the stile and head half left across the field, passing right of willow trees and a pond. Continue on the same line (roughly NW), and go through a gap in the hedge. Pass right of the hedge corner ahead and climb a stile to the A38.

Turn left, cross with care, and before the Nursery, turn right on a bridleway. This runs between hedges, becoming almost a tunnel with some nettle bashing needed in the summer. Go through two gates either side of a track and follow the bridleway downhill as it narrows. After a mile, go through an iron gate and turn left at the edge of a field. At the bottom, go through a gate and turn right to the riverside. Turn left, taking care over an electric fence with barely enough plastic to protect the vitals! Join the riverside path, also the Severn Way. Along this stretch of just over two miles, there are several awkward stiles to negotiate and the cattle are sometimes accompanied by a bull, but there's often no warning sign. So keep your eyes peeled and hope his mind is on other things!

As you approach the town, notice the flood embankment on the left. This helps prevent shallow floods from spreading any further, but once the water has breached this barrier, it takes a long time to drain away. Following the devastating floods of Easter 1998, the area beyond the embankment remained under water for a considerable time and was used as a roost by gulls. Point to Point races are held in Fish Meadow every Easter and August. Go through the underpass gate and rejoin the path back over the bridge.

Walk 23. Waseley and Beacon Hill

Start/parking: Car park at Waseley Country Park, grid reference 972 783. Alternative parking at Beacon Hill, halfway round the walk at grid reference 986 758.

Distance: 5 miles.

Summary: Wonderful walk offering bluebell woodland, open grassy slopes, marvellous views, a wealth of wildlife and a modern "fort". The walk is well waymarked as it follows part of the North Worcestershire Path but it's fairly strenuous with several ups and downs. Some sections can be muddy and there are 10 stiles.

Maps: Landranger 139, Pathfinder 953.

Public transport: Nearest bus stops at Rubery, Frankley, Rednall, Lickey and Romsley Road from Solihull, Bromsgrove and Halesowen. Nearest BR stations at Longbridge and Barnt Green. On Sundays between May and September, a "walkers'" bus from Barnt Green to Kidderminster visits Waseley Country Park on a round trip which includes Lickey, Clent and Kinver.

The Tea Shop

Waseley Hills Café, Waseley Country Park.

The welcoming, airy café with wooden beams has, as its focal point, a wood burning stove. Lynn Round, as you'll recall from Walk 11, also runs the café at the Lickey Hills visitor centre. At Waseley, Julie takes care of the many customers, while the deservedly popular cakes are all home-made by Lynn. The menu includes a substantial all day breakfast and various hot snacks including jacket potatoes. Equally tasty are the pasties, sausages rolls and home-made soup with apple pie and custard filling any remaining corners. Open every day from 10.00am-4.00pm in winter and until 5.30pm in summer. You can buy local books and souvenirs, together with many leaflets on the comprehensive guided walks organised by the Worcestershire Countryside Service. Tel: 01562 711051.

Beacon fort, Lickey Hills Country Park

The Walk

Waseley Country Park is immensely popular with West Midlands residents and during summer weekends, the hills are thronged with visitors. From the car park, go through the gate, left of the Visitor Centre and head uphill, past a pylon to the toposcope on Windmill Hill. Considering how close we are to suburbia, the contrasting panorama of town and countryside is unexpected. The view extends from the Black Country west across the noisy M5 and over the Clent Hills to wooded Abberley Hill and faraway Clee Hill in Shropshire. We can also see our destination, the pine-clad Beacon Hill on the Lickeys. Not immediately obvious is that we are standing on a natural watershed. Rainfall to the east of Windmill Hill runs to the Trent Valley and North Sea while rain to the west flows via the River Salwarpe to the Bristol Channel.

Continue ahead (fence on the right), and by a North Worcestershire Path waymark, turn right through a gap. Pass left of the plantation, keep ahead past a marker post where the return path joins from the right. Drop downhill to go through a gate ahead, under power lines. Go through another gate ahead and follow the path uphill, (trees on the left) and go past a marker post (Fox and Running Trail).

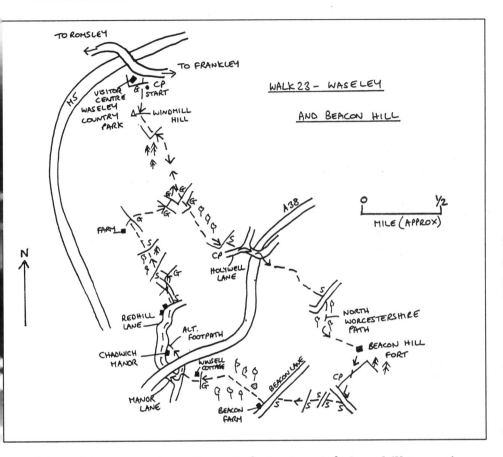

After 100 metres, where the path forks, bear left downhill to us either stile or gate at the bottom. Walk through the car park to the road junction. Turn left down Holywell Lane, and in 50 metres, turn right across a bridge over the A38. At the end, turn right on a bridleway which swings left uphill. The rough lane levels out and at a junction, go left on the N.W. Path. Follow the track alongside a fence to go over a stile to a road.

Cross and turn right over a footbridge uphill on a muddy stretch of the N.W. Path. Climb alongside the golf course and emerge, after much sweat and toil, in sight of the "fort" on top of Beacon Hill, part of the Lickey Hills Country Park. Tremendous views extend across the urban sprawl of Birmingham, with the tree-topped mound of Frankley Beeches particularly prominent. Stand with your back to the fort steps, and head half left across the grass, with conifers away to the left. Halfway along the hedge on the left, go through a gap and turn right on a path alongside the hedge to cross the road. Turn left and in 50 metres, by a National Trust sign, go over a stile on the right. Head half right across the field, cross a stile, then a drive and another stile in quick succession. Walk over the next two fields crossing two stiles, keeping the same line, on a clear path to a lane.

Turn left and by Beacon Farm, turn right down a bridleway, passing right of the buildings to join a muddy path past a stagnant pond. Follow the path downhill through the trees, and a drift of bluebells in the spring. Various bypasses allow you to avoid the worst of the mud. Go through the metal gate at the bottom, pass Winsell Cottage and go down their drive to a lane. Here there is a choice of routes. The footpath to the right past a bus shelter, crosses the A38 and passes Chadwich Manor to join a minor road. But the A38 is a very fast, dangerous dual carriageway and it's less nerve-wracking to follow the road, as I'll now describe. Turn left, and at the T-junction, right along Manor Lane under the A38 and follow the minor road past Chadwich Manor (where the footpath joins the road).

Continue along Redhill Lane, past houses and over a stile on the left into a field. Head half right to join a drive and, after the next hedge-line, turn half right uphill to a kissing gate by a marker post. Head half left to the corner of the wood, cross a stile and walk through the wood. Cross a stile, and head half right uphill to a clearer path passing right of the farm buildings. At the fence beyond the farm, don't cross the stile, but turn right through a gateway uphill on a bridleway. Go through a handgate at the top, back into Waseley Country Park. Walk past the seat, bear left and go through another handgate. Walk ahead and rejoin the outward path past the toposcope to the visitor centre.

Walk 24. Worcester City

Start/parking: Numerous car parks in Worcester but the traffic can be horrendous. It's better to arrive by train and Foregate station is passed on the walk, which starts from the entrance to the Cathedral.

Distance: 4 miles

Summary: A superb circuit of an ancient city, with a wealth of architectural and historical interest. We see the riverside, Cathedral, canal, civil war centre and pass some fascinating buildings. Boots are not needed – but several of the pedestrian crossings are designed for sprinters.

Maps: Landranger 150, Pathfinder 996 but a Worcester street plan from the tourist office is more detailed.

Public transport: Two British Rail stations, Shrub Hill and Foregate (the latter on the route of the walk) and frequent services from all corners including Birmingham, London and Bristol. Numerous buses from all directions.

The Tea Shops

Cloisters Café, Worcester Cathedral

Situated in the cool shade of the cloisters, this atmospheric and cosy tea room is run by volunteers. The café offers a limited but reasonably priced range of tea, coffee and biscuits with a delicious range of home-made cakes, all baked locally by volunteers, together with soup and sandwiches. Open: Saturdays 10.30am-4.00pm in January and February, and Monday to Saturday 10.30am-3.30pm in March, November and December. From April to October, Monday to Saturday 10.30am-5.00pm and 2.30pm-4.30pm on Sunday. Tel: 01905 21004.

Hodson's Coffee House, High Street, Worcester

Overlooking the bustling High Street, with a statue of Elgar standing guard nearby, Hodson's is a deservedly popular venue. Just about every appetite is catered for in its comprehensive menu which offers baguettes, sandwiches and jacket potatoes, all with tempting fillings. Soup, salads, ploughman's, quiches and more substantial hot meals are available. An interesting specials board offers a considerable choice and anyone with a sweet tooth will find it difficult to choose from the tempting array of cakes, puddings and ice cream on offer. Hodson's are holders of a "Clean Food Award" and a "Heartbeat Award Certificate" recognising the choice of healthy food, no smoking and air conditioning in the hotter months. In summer, you can sit at tables outside with a view to the Cathedral. Open all year from Monday to Saturday 9.00am-5.00pm. Tel: 01905 21036.

The Walk

The magnificent structure of Worcester Cathedral dominates every view of the city. Among its many treasures are King John's tomb, a magnificent Norman crypt and a chantry built for Prince Arthur, Henry VIII's elder brother. His death surely marked one of the great crossroads in English history, because, but for a twist of fate, he would have been King instead of Henry. You can buy a fascinating guidebook which covers the history of the Cathedral in far more detail than yours truly has space for, but I can't resist one anecdote. In the 10th century, the good citizens of Worcester dealt out summary justice to a thief who attempted to steal the Sanctus Bell – they flayed him alive and nailed his skin to the cathedral doors!

From the Cloister entrance to the Cathedral, turn right past the Cathedral Ferry sign and down steps to the riverside on Kleve Walk. Notice the flood levels carved into the wall, including the two most recent inundations in 1998. During the summer, you can take boat trips on the river while a ferry shuttles across to the opposite bank where the County Cricket ground boasts one of the most magnificent settings of any sports ground in the country. Turn left alongside the river and soon Kleve Walk becomes Diglis Parade, where Severn Street on the left leads to the Worcester Royal Porcelain Company, one of the city's most popular attractions. A behind the scenes tour allows you to see the entire process and you can also visit the Dyson Perrins Museum which contains one of the world's largest collections of porcelain.

Continue along the river to Diglis Bottom Lock where the Worcester and Birmingham canal joins the Severn. Turn left alongside the canal and walk round the right edge of the marina across several

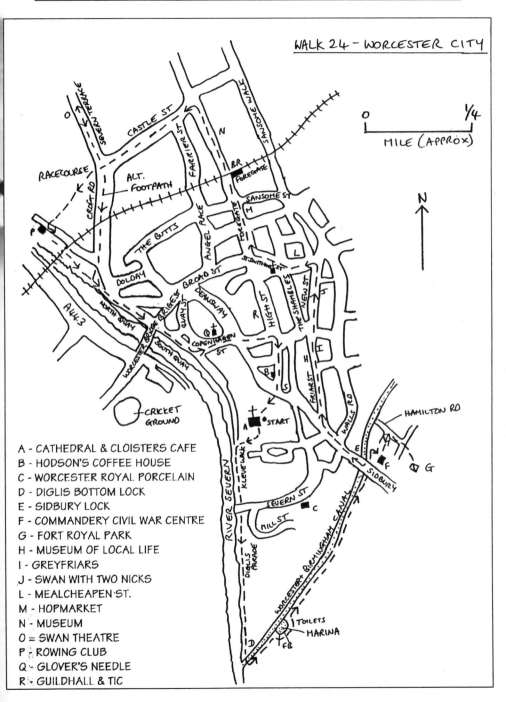

WALK 24 - WORCESTER CITY

A - CATHEDRAL & CLOISTERS CAFE
B - HODSON'S COFFEE HOUSE
C - WORCESTER ROYAL PORCELAIN
D - DIGLIS BOTTOM LOCK
E - SIDBURY LOCK
F - COMMANDERY CIVIL WAR CENTRE
G - FORT ROYAL PARK
H - MUSEUM OF LOCAL LIFE
I - GREYFRIARS
J - SWAN WITH TWO NICKS
L - MEALCHEAPEN·ST.
M - HOPMARKET
N - MUSEUM
O = SWAN THEATRE
P ‡ ROWING CLUB
Q - GLOVER'S NEEDLE
R ‡ GUILDHALL & TIC

footbridges. By the loos, turn left and follow the canal towpath under two bridges to Sidbury Lock at the Commandery. This museum, devoted to England's civil war, is housed in the building used as the Royalist headquarters before the Battle of Worcester. The city can claim connections with both the beginning and end of the civil war. As its motto, "The City Faithful in War and Peace", suggests, Worcester was the first city to declare for the Royalists after the Battle of Powick Bridge in 1642 and the last to surrender at the Battle of Worcester in 1651. The plaque on the canal bridge contains the famous words uttered by a victorious Cromwell, "It is for aught I know a Crowning Mercy".

A short detour to Fort Royal Park is worthwhile. Leave the Commandery via the gardens into Derby Road, turn right along Hamilton Road and enter the park. Climb to the top of the park where you can enjoy superb views to the Cathedral and the blue haze of the Malverns. Return to the front of the Commandery and turn right along the main road, Sidbury. Cross Walls Road, where a safe pedestrian crossing is desperately needed. (The risks involved may account for the handily placed Hospital A & E sign!). Turn right down Friar Street, which becomes pedestrianised as it passes the Museum of Local Life and Greyfriars, a striking timber-framed house in the care of the National Trust.

Continue ahead down New Street past Market Hall and a pub with an intriguing name, The Swan with Two Nicks. Turn left into Cornmarket and Mealcheapen Street and at St Swithin's church, bear half right down St Swithin's Street. Turn right down Foregate passing the Hopmarket. Walk past the end of Sansome Street. Continue under the railway bridge by Foregate Station, past the City Museum and Art Gallery where Queen Victoria's statue looks less than thrilled with life, let alone amused.

Turn left down Castle Street, and cross over before the end to avoid a dangerous junction. Turn right up Severn Terrace (the Swan Theatre is further along). Almost immediately, go left onto the racecourse. Follow the tarmac path across the course to the Rowing Club. (Obviously, you can't use this path on race days, or if the river has flooded the course! If this is the case, turn left from Severn Terrace along Croft Road under the railway and join the riverside path by North Quay). If you have crossed the racecourse, turn left by the river under the railway bridge and along North Quay. Cross Worcester Bridge (another dangerous junction), and continue down South Parade onto South Quay where you can feed the many swans.

Turn left up Copenhagen Street past the spire known as Glover's Needle, a familiar landmark and all that remains of St Andrew's church. At the top, cross the Deansway and walk ahead to the High Street, with the Guildhall and tourist office to the left. Over the doors of the Guildhall is an effigy of Cromwell's head, unceremoniously nailed by the ears and looking more like a pixie than the mighty Lord Protector. Standing either side of him, like a pair of bookends, are the rather smug-looking statues of Charles I and II. Turn right, passing Hodson's Coffee House and Elgar's statue to the Cathedral.

Cloisters, Worcester Cathedral

Walk 25. Wyre Forest

Start/parking: Wyre Forest Visitor Centre, Callow Hill, off A456 grid reference 749739

Distance: 5 miles.

Summary: An ideal introduction to the Wyre Forest on a mixture of good surfaced tracks and muddy footpaths. Don't forget your binoculars to enjoy the wealth of wildlife. Spring highlights include a dazzling display of bluebells while the autumn colours are breathtaking. Oodles of mud but no stiles. On the map, other main paths are shown where they intersect with your route, but bear in mind that the Forest is riddled with paths both major and minor.

Maps: Landranger 138, Pathfinder 952.

Public transport: Regular buses call at Callow Hill for the Visitor Centre from Birmingham, Bewdley, Kidderminster, Ludlow, Leominster and Hereford. Nearest BR station at Kidderminster and the Severn Valley Railway runs to Bewdley.

The Tea Shop

The Pantree, Wyre Forest Visitor Centre.

The open-plan Centre has been divided into a shop and tea room, with the blazing log fire a welcome feature in winter. You can choose from a wide range of baguettes and sandwiches with an interesting variety of fillings. The specials board changes regularly and offers a good choice of pasta, ploughman's, jacket potatoes, salads and soup. A speciality of the Pantree is Commissioners Pie, made from vegetables of the season in a cheese sauce, topped with a pie crust. A delicious selection of cakes and sponge puddings, together with a children's menu, ensures plenty of choice for whatever time of day you visit. The Pantree also holds regular "Round the World" menu days featuring cuisine from different countries. As you eat, you can watch the birds having their lunch at a feeding station in the small garden. Open every day except Xmas from 10.00am-dusk in winter, and to at least 5.00pm in summer. Tel: 01299 266944.

The Walk

Today, as we're deprived of woodland of any significant size, apart from remnants like the New Forest, it's tempting to picture the Wyre Forest as one of our largest. However, it's a mere tenth of its original size. Once a royal hunting forest, the Wyre has supported many industries including boat building and tanning. Deer horns were carved to produce combs, household items and hunting horns. Coppiced oak provided the local market with poles, while charcoal was in great demand during the Industrial Revolution. Much of the Forest is now looked after by Forest Enterprise and several waymarked trails can be followed. In recognition of its value to wildlife, and in an effort to safeguard it for future generations, the Wyre was declared a National Nature Reserve in 1978. Although the Forest is popular with visitors, very few venture far from the car parks and it's possible to wander for hours without seeing a soul.

As well as the unusual conifers, the deciduous woodland is a jumble of oak, birch, beech, ash and hazel and in the far reaches, the trees have an undisturbed, almost Tolkienesque, atmosphere. Coppicing has gradually been reintroduced to selected areas, and you'll see many cleared areas where wildflowers flourish. A huge variety of common flowers grow in profusion and the wood is home to a number of rarities, whose discovery we owe to the 19th century botanist, George Jorden. At the base of many trees are seemingly random mounds of scattered pine needles and leaf litter which form the nests of the Wood Ant, a speciality of the Wyre. The green wood-

Squirrel, Wyre Forest

pecker considers them a delicacy and they are vital to the forest's ecosystem. Feeding on carrion such as dead mice and birds, and killing other insects harmful to trees, they are the cleaners of the forest.

Birdlife is abundant and the Wyre is far enough west to support several species characteristic of sessile oakwoods. Redstart, spotted and pied fly-catchers arrive each summer for an all too brief breeding season. The pied flycatcher, the male in gorgeous black and white evening dress, has benefited enormously from the provision of nestboxes. Another relatively common summer bird is the wood warbler, blessed with a spectacular song, which starts with several clear, high notes and ends with a trill like a spinning coin. If you're lucky enough to catch sight of the bird as it sings, you'll see it put heart and soul into the song with head thrown back, wings spread and every feather quivering. An early morning walk in spring, accompanied by the dawn symphony chorus, will reveal dozens of species of birds. The conifers also support crossbills and the elusive hawfinch, which can sometimes be found feeding beneath the canopy. Wyre is home to a herd of fallow deer but you'll need to move quietly to have a chance of seeing any. Muntjac deer are also fairly common but, being small and sensitive to disturbance, they too can be very elusive.

With the Centre to the left, walk downhill past a "Please ride slowly" sign, on a surfaced track. Follow the red marker posts (ignore other colours), and at a track junction, go left uphill. Emerge onto a tarmac track, turn right, (signed Forest Walks) and ignore the first track to the right. Take the next path right, off the tarmac (red post and yellow arrow), and go past seats and a pond. When the yellow arrow points ahead, turn left (red marker) and along a path to a tarmac track. Turn right and at the next junction, leave the red route to continue ahead downhill. Cross the old railway line by Park House and walk ahead, bearing right downhill to cross the footbridge over Dowles Brook (see Walk 2 for details of this burbling waterway).

Turn right and in 50 metres, go left on a track from the ford. At the next bridge by a pond, turn right past a weight restriction sign. You can judge for yourself whether you can cross safely! Cross the next bridge and climb parallel to Dowles Brook on the left. Where the path returns to stream level and reaches a ford, bear right uphill away from the stream, past a Horseshoe Trail sign. The path swings left alongside a deer fence to the old railway. Turn right along it and at the first crossing track, turn left, past a yellow arrow up to another crossroads. Go straight over and at the next junction, (yellow arrow goes right), continue ahead on a muddy track. This winds through the trees, drops to cross a stream, then climbs and bears right to a cross track. Go straight over, (ignore the next path right), and drop to

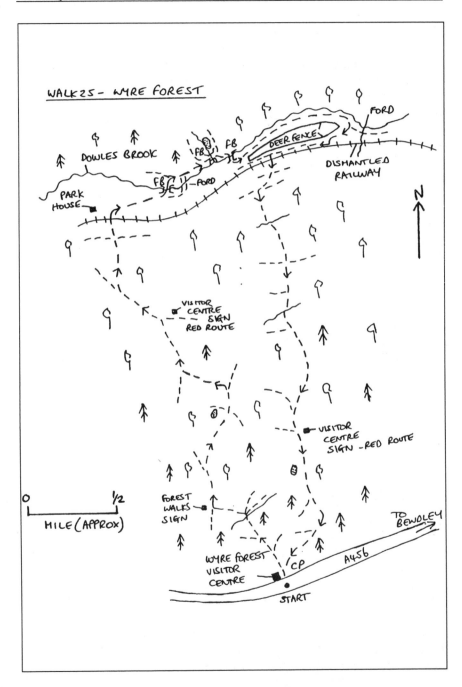

cross another stream. Climb up the other side and keep ahead (ignore a path right).

Continue ahead, with a young plantation on the right. The path becomes grassy, then joins a muddy track. Keep straight ahead to a junction by a signpost to rejoin your old friend, the red marker post. Go straight ahead on a wide track (signed to the Visitor Centre). Follow the red markers uphill past a pond and a cleared area all the way back to the car park. As you get nearer, more coloured rings join the red ones. Remember, the more rings - the nearer you are to the car park and the Pantree!

Tea Shop Walks - Spreading everywhere!

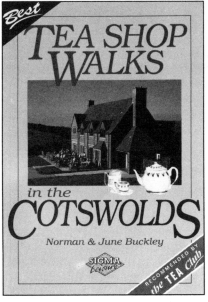

The Sigma Leisure Tea Shop Walks series already includes:

Cheshire

The Chilterns

The Cotswolds

The Lake District, Volume 1

The Lake District, Volume 2

Lancashire

Leicestershire & Rutland

North Devon

The Peak District

Shropshire

Snowdonia

South Devon

Staffordshire

Surrey & Sussex

Warwickshire

The Yorkshire Dales

Each book costs £6.95 and contains an average of 25 excellent walks: far better value than any other competitor!

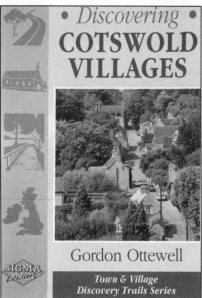